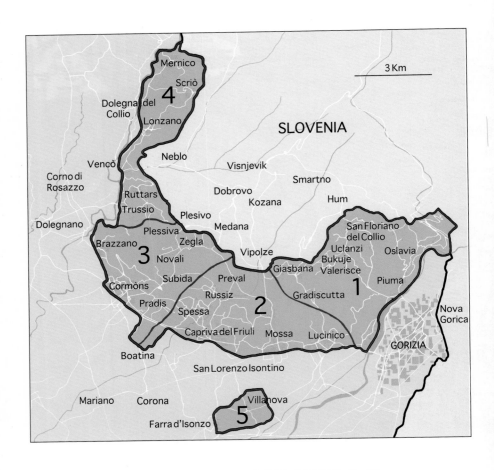

Collio

FINE WINES AND FOODS FROM ITALY'S NORTH-EAST

Collio

Fine wines and foods
from Italy's North-East

Written and
photographed by
Carla Capalbo

PALLAS ATHENE

FOR MY BROTHERS AND SISTERS,
A CREATIVE, SUPPORTIVE, INSPIRING BUNCH:

MARCO CAPALBO

ISABELLE LOUSADA SODOWICK
AND SEBASTIAN LOUSADA

OLIVIA AND JULIAN LOUSADA
SANDRA LOUSADA RICHARDS
AND JENNY LOUSADA WEST

Contents

*Opposite: Orchard
on Monte Quarin
above Cormòns*

*Opposite: Rocks in
Russiz vineyard,
showing the tiny
fossils typical of the
Collio soil*

Preface
by Nicholas Belfrage MW

There are not many hidden gems in the wine world of today, but Friuli's Collio probably comes as close as any to qualifying for the description. As Tuscany, and in particular Chianti Classico, was the centre of Italy's post-war red renaissance, so this small production zone over by the Italian-Slovenian border was the engine room from which Italy's white wines were able to come out of their cheap-and-cheerful past into the light of high quality and desirability. It is a tale of artistry and originality, of dedication to principle over profit, of blends never previously attempted anywhere and wine-making methods which only the boldest would adopt.

Carla Capalbo, a journalist of impeccable objectivity and taste, tells the story through prose and photograph in a style which, following her outstanding books on Tuscany and Campania, can fairly be described as 'inimitable'. Nor does she limit herself to the wines which are perhaps the most salient feature of the zone's creativity, but presents a complete picture which includes artisanal producers of cheeses, prosciutti and other foods, as well as the best places to eat, stay and visit within the area. This book should be viewed as a necessary companion for anyone contemplating a visit to Venice and points east, indeed anyone seeking to bring a fresh new gastronomic experience into their lives.

Opposite:
Chardonnay grapes
at Toros

Foreword

by Lidia Bastianich

Friuli has a very special place in my heart, thirty years after having migrated from my native Trieste to America. I have often returned in my quest for the best wines and regional products and recipes to offer my restaurant's American audience. This area has seen lean times, and its people are frugal yet hospitable, as are its local producers. The Collio, the gentle hills of Friuli under the Alps, is where the best Italian white wines have been produced for years and they nobly accompany the area's foods.

The cuisine of Friuli is rustic and elegant at the same time, seasonal and local. A cauldron of hot bubbling polenta can always be found in most homes and its adornments can range, in spring, from foraged or garden greens to the hearty pork *salumi* found hanging in Collio cantinas and food shops. *Brovada* is an unusual speciality: pickled turnips shredded, pan-sautéed and paired with *musetto*, a deliciously gelatinous pork sausage. Served together, the tartness of the brovada and richness of the musetto create a harmony that marries perfectly with the local Tocai grape, now called Friulano. Go in spring and you'll see women and men in the hills and meadows searching for wild greens: spindly asparagus, nettle shoots, or *sclopit* (*Selene vulgaris* or Bladder Campion), which is tangy, herbal and acidic all in the same bite. These herbs all end up in a great plate of gnocchi, risotto or soup with which the local Pinot Grigio goes so well. Then there is *frico*, baked Montasio cheese with potatoes and onions, usually served with a slab of grilled polenta. The best way to enjoy it is sitting around a *fogolar* with the crackling fire raging. This four-sided open hearth has a central hood from which the polenta cauldron usually hangs.

As in so much of today's world, these romantic traditions are being lost, but if you travel to Friuli and wander off into a village osteria on a cold winter's day, chances are that you will find a fogolar with the fire blazing and something cooking over it. Sitting around its warmth with a group of friends, a slice of crunchy frico and a delicious glass of Collio wine – that's the Friuli I love.

Opposite: Homemade gnocchi di susine are filled with plums

Acknowledgements

This book has come about thanks to the encouragement of the Collio's Consortium and its director, Paolo Bianchi, who first discussed the idea with me several years ago. Its presidents, then and now, Ornella Venica, Paolo Caccese and Patrizia Felluga, were all enthusiastic, as was its honorary president, Marco Felluga. I wish to thank them and the members of the Consortium's council and staff for their support during this project. Everyone in the Consortium's offices in Cormòns, from Alessandro Zanutta and Dario Maurig (in the viticultural sector), to Denis Giorgiutti, Martina Sinigoj, and Giulio Sala (control sector), was very supportive, as was Roberta Medessi, who often helped resolve day-to-day problems. In particular I would like to thank Debora Bonutti who has been a cheerful and patient trip organizer for me, and has handled every bump in the road with good natured generosity; she has made my job a more pleasant and much easier one.

I was left quite free to select and visit the wineries and restaurants I include here, but was given very welcome logistical help in the form of hospitality in some of the Collio's agriturismi and restaurants.

I was fortunate to stay in some lovely wine estates in the many months of 2008 I spent in the Collio. I enjoyed the hospitality of Edi and Silvana Keber and their family, with whom I stayed several times; of Elisabetta Polencic, Ornella Venica and of Zvonka Korsic. My greatest debt is to Savina, Tereza and Renato Keber who not only took me in on many occasions, but offered me the chance to live with them as an adopted family member. Nadia Bianchi was always a welcoming hostess and Beatrice and Nicolò Bianchi were helpful in their occasional roles as photo assistants. They introduced me to the Friulian journalist, Cristina Burcheri, whose knowledge about the history of Gorizia was invaluable.

I would also like to thank Patrick Lucas and Martin Chapman at Beacon Press, for their professionalism and help; Harold Bartram whose original design template for my Campania book this one is modelled on; and the professional labs that developed my film, Colore Due in Milan and Copyright in Naples.

Being on the road as much as I am is only possible thanks to the people who mind the fort back home: Luigina and Giulio Aiello in Pollino, and Anastasia and Aurelio Schiavone in Nusco. Thanks go to Alessandro Porcelli for taking me to Muggia's castle and beyond;

and to Don Dossett for his welcome help with the maps. In Gorizia Richard, Marje, Sarah and Phil Baudains generously shared their Collio experiences with me, and cooked me wonderful dinners. Nick Belfrage and his books on Italian wine have long offered inspiration, as has Fred Plotkin and his fine books on Italian and Friuli gastronomy. Giampaolo Gravina is the person who first introduced me to the Collio, and his enthusiasm and discerning palate got me started on this journey. Claude and Lydia Bourguignon have helped me to see vineyards more critically. My publisher and dear friend, Alexander Fyjis-Walker has encouraged me all the way and been, as ever, a sensitive collaborator and brilliant partner on the visual side of the book. Alison Evans has kept me in great shape, body and soul, with her innovative stretchworks programme, even from afar. Antonietta Scovotto, Silvia Imparato, Jenny and Antonio Pisaniello, Marc De Grazia, Erminia di Meo, Vincenzo D'Alessandro and Maria Teresa Giannarelli have been important long distance friends, as have Jill and Robert Slotover, Lauren Crow, Wallace Heim, Tracy Tynan and Jim McBride, Misette Casano, Nancy Norman Lassalle, Rosemary George and Christopher Galleymore, Tony and Siri Harris, Elizabeth Heyert, Peter Frank and Nicky and John Popham.

Thanks go too to my extended family in America and London for their support, and to my father Carmen Capalbo, in New York, for his. My brother Marco has answered endless long distance questions and stayed in constant touch. My mother, Pat Lousada, has offered everything from delicious meals while we were laying out the book to a home for the winter as I was finishing the texts – as well as an occasional night at the opera to keep me going.

Most of all a great thank you is due to the producers of wines and foods in the Collio and Friuli and their families, who have been so generous with their time, wines and dishes. *Grazie tante a tutti!*

Veronika and Tereza Keber

How to use this book

THE COLLIO AND HOW THE BOOK IS ARRANGED

The Collio is a small crescent-shaped area within the province of Gorizia, in the region of Friuli Venezia Giulia, on Italy's border with Slovenia. The Collio is situated within eight of the province of Gorizia's 25 comuni, or townships, and their surrounding countryside: Gorizia, San Floriano del Collio, Mossa, Capriva del Friuli, San Lorenzo Isontino, Cormòns, Dolegna del Collio and Farra d'Isonzo. To facilitate the wine enthusiast's travels, this book has divided the Collio into five chapters. Chapters 1, 2 and 3 are limited to the Collio vineyards and the towns adjacent to them, while chapters 4 and 5 take us from the Collio's vineyards to explore some of the restaurants, food artisans and cultural sites within the western and southern parts of the region of Friuli Venezia Giulia, as far as the sea and its great capital city and port, Trieste. Since the book is focused on Gorizia and its territories, the book begins there and proceeds across the Collio – and then Friuli – in a counter-clockwise direction.

THE MAPS

Each chapter begins with a detailed map of the Collio showing the area's towns, villages and vineyard *crus*, such as Russiz or Zegla; usually these correspond to local names for a specific sub-zone, hillside or wood. The scale is very small, and allows the traveller to locate the 61 individual wineries profiled in the book. Restaurants and food artisans are listed by the town in which they are found. The order of the wineries follows a hypothetical journey from Gorizia through the territory of the Collio from east to west, south to north. Chapters 4 and 5 also feature larger maps. Any town in which a restaurant entry appears is underlined; these towns are listed in a counter-clockwise order, beginning in Chapter 4 northeast of Udine at Montefosca, and ending in Chapter 5 with Trieste. Local maps are available from Friuli Venezia Giulia's tourist offices, but if you plan to do much driving get Touring Club Italiano's (green-covered) 1:200,000 map of the region as it shows the smaller roads in detail. The Collio Consortium also provides a map locating its key members.

Opposite: Montefosca's dairyman, Giuliano Cernet, with cheese

THE ENTRIES

This book focuses on wineries, restaurants, food artisans and agriturismi. The word agriturismo covers places to sleep and eat on wine estates and farms. Many function exclusively as Bed & Breakfasts; others only operate as rural trattorias; I've indicated which category they come under in the text. Food artisans are listed by the food they produce.

Each entry provides the address and telephone number of the business, with internet addresses where available. In Italy, the house numbers are written after the street name.

THE WINE ENTRIES

This book gives an overview of the Collio's history and unique winemaking capacities. It profiles 61 quality wine estates within the Collio, and lists an additional 54, all members of the Collio Consortium. This book is a collection of the personal histories of some of the key estates. Rather than focus always on detailed tasting notes, I've adopted a free-form approach to my visits, and written about different aspects of Collio winemaking in each case. The wine estates I have written about vary in length; reduced length does not imply that the products or producers are less interesting – I just didn't have space or time to write more. Nor does not being profiled or photographed in the book imply that a winery or restaurant is not good: I hope to enlarge the list in future editions. In the listings, the wine entries are alphabetized by the key word in their company titles.

There is no substitute for the experience of tasting a fine wine in the cellars that made it. Wines may be bought directly from most estates at prices that are the same or slightly lower than nearby wine shops. At all but the biggest wineries (which may have permanent staff on hand to show you around), it is always best to phone ahead to arrange a visit. All are hospitable and keen on receiving interested visitors—novices and experts alike—so don't miss out on this exciting opportunity.

THE RESTAURANT REVIEWS

I don't give scores or points in my wine or restaurant reviews: this is not an 'objective' book written by a nondescript person posing as a travelling salesman. I'm recognizable and well known in Italy, and couldn't have remained anonymous even if I'd wanted to. The idea is to give a sketch of the places I visit and get to know the chefs and owners – that's the part I find interesting. I like all kinds of restaurants. This does not mean that I haven't used a critical eye, or palate, when eating in them. I describe the food I have eaten and the season of my visit.

I have reviewed restaurants in all price ranges and styles. Some specialize in traditional cuisine, others take a more modern approach. These are necessarily subjective accounts – the rest is up to you.

The PRICE CATEGORY is used only for restaurants, and it gives the average cost per person of a three- or four-course meal without wine, beverages, or service and cover charges (prices accurate as of January 2009). Obviously, meals based on snacks or fewer courses will cost less, so these price ranges should be used as a guide only. It is often a good idea to choose the *menu degustazione* – or tasting menu – in which several courses are offered for a predetermined price.

€ up to 18 Euros
€€ 18–26 Euros
€€€ 26–38 Euros
€€€€ 38–52 Euros
€€€€€ 52–72 Euros
€€€€€€ 72 Euros and over

OPENING HOURS In northern Italy lunch is usually between 12.30 and 14.30, but it's best to be at table by 13.30 at the latest. Dinner is from 19.30 to 21.30; again, try to sit down by 21.00 or phone to check what time the kitchen shuts. Shops close from 12.30 or 13.00 for one to two hours; they close between 17.00 and 20.00.

GLOSSARY Translations of Italian and Slovenian food and wine terms commonly used in the Collio and in this book. The glossary also will help in translating menus found in the area.

INDEX At the end of the book you'll find several indexes: of wineries; restaurants; agriturismi and other places to stay; and a more general index of place and personal names and other subjects.

PHOTOGRAPHS A word about the images in this book. They are all photographs taken by me for this project, using colour slide film and three vintage Nikon cameras with a handful of lenses – nothing digital! They were laid out by Alexander Fyjis-Walker and me. The picture-taking was done as and when I could: there was a lot of rain in 2008, so some producers were simply not photographed because of lack of light or time.

TRAVEL INFORMATION For more information contact www.collio.it and www.turismofvg.it. There are excellent overnight train services from London to Venice, and thence to Gorizia, with no baggage limit. Motorail services are also available to Villach, close by over the Austrian border, or to Verona, via Düsseldorf. The Aeroporto Friuli-Venezia Giulia is at Ronchi dei Legionari outside Trieste, and there are airports at Treviso, Venice and Verona.

Introduction

At a time when globalization and the world's mass markets increasingly threaten to erase all traces of individuality and place-specific character, it has been a pleasure to dive into the small but complex world of the Collio, with its diverse cultural, ethnic and gastronomic realities – that often come together, not surprisingly, around its wines. In the last twenty years, the wines of the Collio have made giant strides and its whites are now recognized as being among Italy's finest, offering fine fruit with enough structure and acidity to age well too.

I hope this book will help the Collio's wines to become better known and encourage readers to visit and enjoy the beauty of its landscapes, the natural pace of its seasons and their fruits, and the genuine hospitality of its people.

POSITIONING THE COLLIO

This book began with a very precise objective: to explore the small but surprisingly diverse wine-producing area in northeastern Italy called, in Italian, il Collio Goriziano. The Collio hills are in the region of Friuli Venezia Giulia, a hundred kilometres north-east of Venice and forty north of Trieste, in the very top right-hand corner of Italy. To its north are the dramatic craggy mountains of the Giulian Alps, while to the south the land flattens out completely towards the Adriatic sea, just thirty-five kilometres away. The croissant-shaped collar of land in the province of Gorizia called the Collio is bounded to the west by the river Judrio, to the south by the Isonzo river plain, and to the east by Slovenia, the former eastern-block country whose entry into Europe was celebrated at the end of 2007. In terms of wine topography, the Collio DOC is sandwiched between the Colli Orientali del Friuli DOC to its west, the Isonzo DOC to the south and, on the Slovenian side, Brda. There, the hills that form the Collio continue to rise in an area whose winemaking and touristic potential is enormous – but that's the subject of another book.

Opposite: View from Ruttars towards Slovenia, with old-style Casarsa-trained vines in the foreground

*Ponca soil crumbles
in the hand*

*Diagonal layers of
flysh*

The Collio's gentle slopes are beautiful: they're covered primarily with terraced vineyards interspersed with thick patches of woods, fruit orchards and fields – a model of biodiversity. Twenty kilometres long, and barely four across at its widest, the Collio has long been recognized as one of Italy's most prestigious winemaking areas, especially for white wines – something for which Italy has little reputation compared to its great and famous reds. The Collio may be small, but it contains 1,500 hectares of vineyards. None of its hills rise very high: most Collio vineyards are situated between 80 and 200 metres above sea level. That it produces fine wines is no accident: the Collio Goriziano is an important cru for vine-growing thanks to a unique terroir which gives character to any wines that are made on it, whatever their style, colour or grape varieties.

On my first trip to the Collio some years ago I was taken to a vineyard at Russiz, in the heart of the Collio near Cormòns, and shown the miniscule fossils (*nummulites*) that are one of the Collio's most influential features. 'Fifty million years ago a vast ocean floor and coral reef were progressively filled with silt and clay before being pushed up from under the waters as the Alps began to be formed,' explained Paolo Bianchi, the Consortium's director. 'They became limestone mountains that were gradually worn down into the hills we now see. In parts they were filled in with marine sediments, and with hard sands *(arenaria)* and softer silt *(marna)*. That's why this soil breaks up and crumbles with heat or rain. This layering of different soil types is called "flysh" and it's the secret ingredient behind our wines.' Indeed the minerality that this complex soil structure gives is the Collio's defining factor. Some areas have red, acidic soils; in others the soil – also known as *ponca* – is heavily alkaline. It doesn't react well to rain: on slopes its top layers quickly get washed away, whereas on flat land it turns to mud so thick that no tractor can enter the vineyards. That's one reason why so many of the Collio's winemakers plant grass between alternate if not between every row of vines. With grass underfoot, the vineyards remain a little more accessible in wet weather and are less likely to be stripped of their topsoil.

Mineral-rich soil is not the Collio's only bonus for vine growing. The Collio also benefits from being sandwiched between cool winds from Russia and warm air currents from the sea: it's always about three degrees hotter here than further inland, yet there's usually enough breeze to keep the grapes dry. This push and pull of hot and cold, humid and dry winds is a vital aspect of the microclimate here, as is the protection, like a good solid shoulder, afforded from too many cold northerly winds by the Giulian Alps. The Collio terrain allows for different sub-zones – Zegla, Pradis, Oslavia and Plessiva among them – that can be likened to Burgundy's crus;

Harvest at Zegla

between them, they favour a range of grape varieties. Of course the Collio also produces reds – some of which are excellent – but in the main it is the whites which drive the area's markets and reputation. These whites are an exciting bunch of characters. In an unusual rainbow of styles, white wines in the Collio go from pale and ephemeral, through soft and rich gold, to amber-coloured liquids whose structures are closer to red wines.

This is thanks to the most important element of all, the human factor. The Collio has long been a breeding ground for brilliant winemakers bent on innovation. The 20th century saw a succession of producers able to redefine the idea of Italian white wines, from Douglas Attems and Mario Schiopetto to Nicola Manferrari, Livio and Marco Felluga and Josko Gravner, to name but a few. You'll find their individual stories and contributions to this ongoing wine evolution in the pages of this book. As in the Langhe area of Piemonte, many of the Collio's estates are small, family run affairs. At harvest time, several generations of a family pick and press the grapes; it is their intimate relationship with the vineyards that is reflected in the divergent approaches to making wine you find in the Collio.

HISTORY OF THE
COLLIO: A BRIEF
SURVEY

Culturally and politically, the Collio offers an equally rich mix of influences. It's always been positioned at a crossroads between east and west, north and south. The ancient Romans built Aquileia, a key trading city for which wine was a key commodity, just thirty

Collio cherries

kilometres away near the sea; Pliny and other writers described the wines of these hills in which affluent Romans built villas and farms. The area's wines were important to each of the ruling powers over the next 1500 years, from the Goths and Longobards to the Venetian republic. Documents from 1307 cite a wine tax in Gorizia, where the drink was so popular there was official concern about too much drunkenness. In the past two centuries, this strip of land formed part of the Austro-Hungarian empire until 1915; its final position as Italian was not determined until 1947. Slavic culture too has played an important part here, and continues to do so. Grapes and other warmer-climate crops were always grown in these hills: this was the southernmost part of the Austro-Hungarian empire and the Collio supplied it with wine, cherries and other fruits.

Sadly, the strategically placed hills were never peaceful for long. During the First World War such violent battles were fought along the front lines positioned in the Collio that at Oslavia human bones continue to surface on what is now called Monte Calvario; not a tree was left standing by the end of the war. After the Second World War, the hills were split between Italy and Yugloslavia. During the Cold War, the borders were closely patrolled, with armed guards in vineyards that were now half in Italy, half in what was, in 1992, to become Slovenia. 'We were allowed into Slovenia during the day,' explains Renato Keber, a winemaker whose estate is at Zegla, just inside the Italian border, 'but at night a curfew forced us to return to the Italian side.'

Since Slovenia's official entrance into the Schengen area in January 2008, the border sentries have been removed. You no longer have to show a passport to drive into Slovenia to buy cheaper petrol or to visit the pretty villages with their small farms, wineries and restaurants. There is a strong sense of two cultures living peacefully together: on the Italian side, many families speak Slovenian and town names are written in both languages. Hopefully the next few years will see ever more interchange between the two halves of what was once a single agricultural area.

GRAPE VARIETIES: The Collio's *disciplinare* – or production code – allows for eighteen
INTRODUCTION   official wines to qualify for DOC status: twelve white, four red and two blends. Of these, most are single-varietal wines, with the two Collio '*uvaggi*', or blends being the exception: Collio Bianco DOC and Collio Rosso DOC. The disciplinare specifies the grape varieties allowed to be used in its portfolio of wines, the most important of which are discussed below. If, in the past, the grapes were trained to the traditional Casarsa, Cappuccina and Silvoz and other systems that allowed for huge quantities to be produced from

each vine, modern viticulture favours far less production – ideally circa 1 to 1.5 kilos of fruit per plant – in vineyards planted closely, with from 5,000 to 8,000 thousand plants per hectare. Most are now trained to Guyot or cordon spur, and are subject to annual green pruning to reduce the quantities of bunches and concentrate each vine's energy into less fruit.

WHITES

If wines have historically been made here for centuries, if not millennia, two native grape varieties have been identified with the Collio at least since the Middle Ages: Malvasia Istriana and Ribolla Gialla.

Malvasia Istriana originates in Greece but is prevalent throughout Italy and has been in Friuli since the 14th century when it is thought to have been introduced by the Venetian republic. Although Malvasia is sometimes known as a dessert wine, in the Collio it is at its best dry, and does particularly well in the area of Pradis, where it attains structure and perfume. On the vine, Malvasia can be a gangly affair, with long, loosely formed bunches that sometimes have problems reaching full maturity. In the glass it can be lightly perfumed in a floral way, with hints of salt and pepper; it contributes aromatic character to blends. It is often too low in acidity to last well, though some producers do make it with enough crispness and minerality to age. Malvasia is good as an aperitivo and goes well with fish risotto and with soups.

Left, Grape vine shoots; right, Ribolla Gialla

Ribolla Gialla has been grown in the Collio for centuries, and has long been one of the trio of native grapes (with Malvasia and Tocai Friulano) used in traditional blends, adding a fine acidic vein to the mix. For some, Ribolla Gialla has the potential to become the Collio grape *per eccellenza*: indeed, producers such as Gravner have committed themselves wholeheartedly to this ancient native variety, to the exclusion of all others. To be at its best it requires poor, hilly terrains, strict bunch reduction (some producers even cut away half of each bunch on the vine to concentrate flavour and sugars) and good maturity. At Oslavia, Ribolla has been at the centre of the rebirth of the millenia-old maceration techniques that see the wine left on the skins for up to several months. With maturity, the grapes gain complexity of flavour, tannins and structure, as well as ageing potential. Even in hot summers Ribolla Gialla – so–called for its warm, yellow colour – retains good acidity and *freschezza*; it is often added to blends for these characteristics. It is adaptable and can also be made into refreshing clean, dry wines that are pleasant to drink young as a light *aperitivo* or summer wine.

Tocai Friulano is, from 2007-2008, Tocai no longer – it is now officially called 'Friulano' – yet it's a hard habit to lose as the name is evocative of so much of the area's viticultural history (especially when, to my mind, 'Friulano' is such a bland adjective and could apply to anything male from Friuli). Indeed, many Collio winemakers now consider Tocai the most 'typical' of their native grapes and feel bitter at its loss. If you can muster some Italian, Cristina Coari has written a fine book – or eulogy to it – called 'Bye Bye Tocai', which retraces the whole fiasco of how the Italians failed to fight for the right to keep the name of a grape that had been theirs from at least the 14th century (instead, Hungary won the battle of the Tokayj or Tokaji name for its wine made from the Furmint grape). The Tocai grape is more likely kin to Sauvignonasse, but the jury is still out on that. In a novel twist, Stanko Radikon coined the term 'Jakot' for his wines from the grape, being Tokaj backwards.

Whatever the name, Tocai grapes are grown throughout the Collio, with particularly good results at Zegla, Russiz and Brazzano, where the vines love the *ponca* soils. Tocai has not always been considered a premium grape: the little glasses, or *tajut*, of wine that the ubiquitous osterie of the area once offered were invariably simple, if not rustically made, plonk from this grape, often blended with a bit of Sauvignon to give it character. All that has changed as recent generations of winemakers have applied new thinking and techniques to this variety, with strict bunch selection in the vineyards, later harvesting and better cellaring. The Tocai Friulano vine likes sunny, open positons; the riper it gets, the trickier it is to harvest as it can 'turn' and drop almost overnight. The

Tocai Friulano

Opposite: Tocai Friulano harvest at Ronco della Chiesa, Borgo del Tiglio

results are some of the Collio's most applauded wines, with its straw-yellow hues, delicate bouquet and signature light almond aftertaste. For the Friulani (the real ones, the people), Tocai and prosciutto di San Daniele form a marriage made in heaven, but it also goes well with many local dishes, including frittate and, unusually, the bitter radicchio.

Picolit is not common in the Collio, but a handful of producers do make a dessert wine from it. The Picolit grape is easy to spot: it suffers from what the Italians have named *'aborto floreale'*, or floral abortion, when some of each bunch's flowers fail to pollinate owing to the low fertility of its pollens, leaving uneven quantities of berries to mature. Aromatic, sweet but with a fine acidity, it's worth tasting if you're in the area.

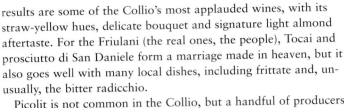

Picolit

The so-called 'international' varieties are mostly French or German (Muller Thurgau, Traminer and Renano). They've been grown in the Collio and areas of Friuli since Napoleonic times. Some, like Chardonnay, were introduced at the end of the 19th century to restock the vineyards after the deadly phylloxera scourge destroyed Italy's vines. Credit must be given to the Count de La Tour who began experimenting at Capriva in the late 19th century with French varieties he brought from Burgundy (see p. 130). Suffice it to say that today, Chardonnay, Sauvignon Blanc and Pinot Grigio are among the most popular varieties in the Collio, with small but very successful amounts of the elegant Pinot Bianco too. In some cases, certain varieties are known to favour particular crus: if Sauvignon does best in the high, cool vineyards of Dolegna and San Floriano, Pinot Grigio is happy on the north- and east-facing slopes below Plessiva. Pinot Grigio is, however, grown throughout the Collio, and is open to interpretation: from steely, crisp whites it can be made, with longer time on the skins, into the copper-hued, or *ramato* wines that were popular in ages past and are now being 'rediscovered'.

Sauvignon

COLLIO BIANCO
DOC

Although most wines in the Collio are declaredly single-varietal, the Collio's signature white wine is the blend called, appropriately enough, Collio Bianco. Historically a blend was made in the Collio from the three native varieties, Ribolla Gialla, Malvasia and Tocai. At the DOC's outset, the orginal intention was to allow certification only for those made from the three grapes grown within the same vineyard. This proved to be too limiting so, in 1992, the Consortium's president Douglas Attems changed the disciplinare to allow for a blend of any of the white grapes specified in it, from any number of registered vineyards.

Thus the current Collio Bianco DOC allows for the French

*The harvest at
Russiz Superiore*

varieties too. Indeed, I find this blend exciting precisely because it is like a blank canvas onto which each producer can create his or her own image of the best the territory can bring, with the added complexity that a well-made blend can offer. Equal freedom is exercised with the vinification techniques. So the range includes selections aged in steel or wood, from native and/or international varieties. Some producers have chosen not to make a Collio Bianco at all, saying they feel it's too vague and misleads drinkers who don't know what to expect from it. Others believe in it so strongly they produce nothing but the Collio Bianco, Patrizia Felluga being one of these (see p. 95). My advice is to sample the Collio Bianco blend from any producer whose wines you admire: that's a good way to start appreciating these diverse and unique wines.

REDS

Pignolo

Despite the emphasis of the Collio's output – circa 80 percent – being focused on white wines, the area does of course also produce some fine reds. On the whole they fail to attain the pinnacles reached by the *vini bianchi*, but there are some exceptions. Of the varieties most present, it is the French Merlot and Cabernet Franc (with a little Pinot Nero) that take precedence. More unique and interesting, however, are the local varieties, Pignolo, Refosco, as well as a small amount of Schioppettino which, however is not recognized in the Collio's *disciplinare*. Pignolo is one of Friuli's key native reds, known for its big structure, tannins and personality; it is grown with success in other parts of the region. Recently it has begun to be reconsidered within the Collio too. It's a wine that softens and improves with age, when it can offer complexity and style.

Ageing Collio Wines
by Richard Baudains

Richard Baudains is a British wine critic who has lived in Gorizia for 20 years, so he's a long-time enthusiast of the Collio and its wines. I asked him about the ageing potential of the Collio's white wines.

'When I first came to Gorizia, in 1989, I made contact with the Consorzio, whose director and technical advisor then was Albano Bidasio. His credo was: "a great wine production area is one that can show five vintages at any one time." That was a very progressive position to take. Even then, the wines had the potential to age well but it was very hard to promote mature or aged wines in Italy, especially if they were white: there's no mystique about whites. In those days, if you had the chance to taste an old vintage it was probably the result of an accidental ageing, because a wine had been left in the cellar unsold: no one collected old vintages of white wines, and producers didn't sell them. In those days whites were bottled by March in readiness for Vinitaly and for the seaside resorts. That's why it was amazing that Mr. Bidasio saw the potential in older wines: he was insightful and innovative.

What enables the Collio whites to age so well? Their extract and structure. At that time, œnologists believed that white wines needed huge acidity to last – along French models – but that's never been the characteristic of Collio wines. In the early 1980s, a wine required 4.5 grams of acidity to be granted the DOC. Sometimes wines made by Gravner and others had to be declassified as they didn't reach that level of acidity. Even without that much acidity the Collio wines go on forever, I think because they are well made from good ripe fruit, with a super balance of alcohol and extract. So it's not just that the wine keeps fresh but that it evolves, improves and develops the bouquet which is the real reason to age a wine anyway. What makes an older white wine so interesting is the complex nose that develops.

Another important aspect of this ageing process is that the Collio wines barely show their potential in the first year or even by the

September following the harvest. Indeed, they are only just starting to show by the next year. So it's positive that some producers now bottle in September and bring their wines out in January instead of June; that's a trend that gives the wines a bit longer to express themselves. A handful of producers – such as La Castellada, Renato Keber, Il Carpino, Gravner, Radikon, or Roberto Felluga's riservas – are an exception that bring some of their wines out at least one full year after the others, if not more. These are often whites that are made like red wines.

In particular it is the native varieties here that age well, whereas the aromatic varieties, such as Sauvignon, tend usually to become a bit static over time. Tocai Friulano is not for the long haul, but does well through five or seven years, whereas Pinot Bianco can come into its own over time, yet is often undervalued when young. That is one of the great things about the Collio Bianco, or white blend, project: it enables very good ageing potential. I think it certainly makes sense for a quality wine-producing region to have one wine that represents that aspect; it's a real innovation.

This Collio Bianco project demonstrates that the varieties are not the whole story, and in that way it's revolutionary. In all this, it's the Collio's terroir that comes through. Whether the wines are oaked or unoaked, made in amphoræ or cement tanks, the grapes are able to take their energy from the Collio's soils. And that's what makes their unique character.

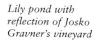

Lily pond with reflection of Josko Gravner's vineyard

The Consorzio Collio and its role today

FOR MORE INFORMATION:
Consorzio Tutela Vini Collio
Via Gramsci, 2
Cormòns
TEL 0481 630303
www.collio.it

The Collio Consortium – Consorzio Tutela Vini Collio – was founded in 1964 by Douglas Attems (see p.103), who wanted to set up an institution to safeguard and promote the Collio as a *denominazione* with a recognizable territorial brand. He served the Collio Goriziano and its DOC (Denominazione di Origine Controllata, first granted in 1968) for over thirty years as president of the Consortium, and was the driving force behind many of its most important early strategic decisions: to delineate the Collio's boundaries around its hillsides rather than the nearby plains; to create a separate DOC Collio, as distinct from a less selective 'Friuli' zone, which might compromise its high-quality image; to work to help the whole Collio area improve its quality, rather than focusing only on its leading estates; to offer technical assistance to its members as the best way to bring this improvement about. Thanks to his vision, the Collio was quickly able to establish itself as one of Italy's best producing areas of quality wines, especially white wines.

Today, an important aspect of the Consortium's work continues to be to advise its members on viticultural and vinification techniques. The Consortium's viticulture team, led by Alessandro Zanutta, with help from Dario Maurig, is constantly updating its information and keeping abreast of new trends and ideas in winemaking. Sandro Zanutta explains: 'Twenty years ago the Consortium, with its external consultant, Paolo Antoniazzi, set up a centre of technical assistance for its members. The then president, Douglas Attems, was committed to improving the standards of winemaking here across the board. He introduced weather charting – of rainfall, humidity, temperature, wind and sun – which gives a useful picture of the way each season is developing and allows for pre-emptive action against fungal and pest attacks to the vines. We are keen to gradually reduce the use of pesticides and weedkillers, but must also guarantee that our growers do not lose their crops, so we try to strike a balance in what is known as *la lotta guidata*, a "guided" fight against the vine's problems. Originally posters were the best way to spread the word but nowadays email is faster and

Winter pruning is always carried out by hand

more direct.' Bulletins contain suggestions about which products to use when, and explore the pros and cons of treatments. New experiments to reduce the use of harmful chemicals and toxins include tractor-sprayers which catch and recycle excess liquids before they reach the ground, and can save up to 80 percent of the products and half of the petrol of older systems.

'Another key area of our collaboration with members is in designing new vineyards,' continues Zanutta. 'This is highly specialized as it needs to take account of earthworks, drainage, orientation, and grape varieties. With these terrains, we have to plan carefully to avoid soil being washed away each time it rains. That's why the current idea is to build vineyards using a series of small terraces 60 to 80 centimetres wide that don't alter the land's topography much but do help against erosion.' The Consortium also sponsors a number of experimental vineyards for trying out new ideas about a series of viticultural practises, including canopy control and grass-planting between the rows. There are also hands-on courses for members on pruning and bud selection which also help reduce illnesses and treatments.

As of January 2009, the Consortium has 168 memberrs, of whom 39 are solely vine-growers, 118 bottlers, nine who make wine but don't bottle it, and two honorary members. Its president is Patrizia Felluga.

The yellow Vespa is a recent promotion that has become synonymous with the Collio – ridden here by Caterina Felluga

The Collio through the eyes of an Italian wine critic

by Giampaolo Gravina

In recent decades the Collio has instilled itself in the minds of Italian consumers as being one of the country's top denominations. Its white wines are known to be among Italy's best, offering character, complexity, and ageing potential. However I suspect that, outside of Italy, this recognition is somewhat lacking, that the word 'Collio' does not yet instantly conjure up an image of excellence and dependability, and that the multitude of wines and grape varieties that each Collio producer has in their portfolio may not yet be perceived as a positive resource.

As the Italian critic Luigi Veronelli reminded us, the Collio's whites are fascinating for their 'variation'. Indeed, it's hard to imagine another winemaking area capable of offering such a range of styles and varieties. From the most innocuous Chardonnay to the macerated, almost tannic Ribolla, here all variations on a theme of white are possible. Each time I taste them, the wines' very personal stories come alive in tones and inflections that suggest a common motif. I'm never left with the impression of simply-reached solutions or unconsidered choices that are frequent now in Italy's chameleon-like wine world. Quite the reverse: it seems that in the Collio there's an organic core, a common texture or 'musical liquidity', as Veronelli described it, that suggests a territorial matrix.

There, I've said it. I'd promised myself not to use the word 'territorio', one of the most over-used in today's wine lexicon, but I've succumbed. How can I suggest the expressive horizon that links so many of the Collio's whites without mentioning the common thread that unites its diverse soils? Malvasia, Pinot Grigio, Friulano, Ribolla, even Sauvignon wines from the Collio often present perfumes and flavours that go beyond those usually associated with an individual variety. In the Collio each type of grape has found an affinity with the terroir of a specific zone, and this coupling produces memorable results: the Malvasia of Pradis, the Ribolla from Oslavia or Sauvignon from San Floriano and Dolegna. Each with its own well-defined personality but all united by the energy and unmistakable depth of flavour that the Collio's soils provide.

Opposite: Zegla vineyards in the early autumn

Eating in the Collio

Slices of prosciutto di San Daniele

The food you find in the Collio reflects, as you'd imagine, its history and varied ethnic influences. On local restaurant menus you're as likely to find Hungarian goulash – or *gulasch* as it's written here – and Slovenian *cevapcici* as pasta or minestrone. (For translations of some of the most common dishes, see the Glossary, p. 247). The Friulian staple is polenta, white or yellow, fine-grained or coarse; in the Isonzo and Natisone valleys where it grows it accompanies everything, from fish to cheese and vegetables. I found the most popular Collio dish to be gnocchi. Not the small, bite-sized potato gnocchi of central Italy, but challenging potato and flour dumplings as big as lemons. They're at their best filled with plums *(prugne)* and sprinkled with sugar and cinnamon as starters or desserts. The legacy of the Austro-Hungarian era is felt at every course, from hearty meat dishes of game and beef to the ubiquitous strudels filled with apples and raisins. A local speciality is *la Gubana*, a spiral cake stuffed with nuts and raisins.

The Adriatic contributes a colourful cast of sea-creatures to restaurants specializing in seafood. 'Land' and 'sea' dishes rarely coincide in the same kitchens, with the exception of those of high gastronomy chefs such as Emanuele Scarello at Agli Amici (p. 206) who is comfortable with both. In the simple osterie and trattorie that abound in the Collio and beyond, the classic pattern is to begin with mixed salumi – home-cured pork *salame* and prosciutto – and then have gnocchi, a pasta dish or soup, followed by assorted meats grilled over a wood fire, with desserts to follow. The food is usually hearty and uncomplicated. *La brovada*, grated pickled turnips, accompany fatty pork jowl sausages in a classic peasant combination. Indeed, winter showcases the pig in all its glory: I was amazed to discover that many family wineries still fatten one or two pigs each year for home use, to have delicious sausages and cured meats to offer guests with a glass of wine. In the Collio as in the rest of Italy, wine is never drunk on its own. Even before dinner it always accompanies a slice of ham, a chunk of cheese, some breadsticks and olives. The idea is not to guzzle it down, but to savour the wine in the company of friends, with well-made food to accompany it.

Opposite: 'snow in a glass' – a winter dessert at Sale e Pepe

Olive oil in the Collio

Around the Mediterranean, grape vines and olive trees often co-exist and favour the same types of climate and soils. The Collio offers the olive tree one of its northernmost growing areas in south-facing hills whose latitude is tempered by warm winds from the sea. Historical records and oral accounts attest to the olive's past role in the area's landscape: an 18th-century map of the Conti Formentini estate shows an olive grove situated amongst the vineyards. The extremely cold winter of 1763 – similar to the 1985 freeze that killed most of central Italy's olive trees – devastated the Collio's groves. Gorizia's agricultural superintendents replied by sponsoring local farmers to the tune of four florins for every 25 olive trees planted in the 1770s as a means of regenerating oil production. Another cyclical freeze occurred in the winter of 1929, this time causing the almost total elimination of olive trees from the Collio's territory. It has only been recently – in the 1980s – that the olive tree has begun to make a comeback on both the Italian and Slovenian sides of the border.

Today several indigenous varieties such as Bianchera, Carbona and Drobnizza are found alongside the better-known southern-Italian olive cultivars. As yet few Collio producers are producing large quantities of extra virgin olive oil, but those who have begun include Russiz Superiore, Alessio Komjanc and Livon.

Olive trees grow among the vines at Komjanc's winery

Festivals in and around the Collio

These are the most important festivals, and those that have to do with food and wine, though others exist and can be found at the region's website www.turismofvg.it or in the brochure about them: *Gustare il Territorio.*

Capriva
Michele Grion's folklore group organizes events throughout the year. www.folkcapriva.it

Cividale del Friuli
Mittelfest (July): An internationally renowned avant-garde festival of theatre, music, dance and art, with special events in the town's restaurants too. www.mittelfest.org

Palio di San Donato (August): Medieval food, markets and tournaments in period costume transform this lovely town into a period spectacle. www.cividale.net

Cormòns
La Viarte (May): In the Collio's favourite event, La Viarte – which means 'spring' in Friulano – brings the town and Monte Quarin to life with food, wine, games and music presented in sixteen Cormòns courtyards, from Sunday morning till night. www.comune.cormons.go.it

Genetliaco (August): Costumed re-enactment of the crowning of Emperor Franz Joseph (Francesco Giuseppe) in 1848, when the area was united in a single state.

Rievocazione Storica (August): On a Sunday in late August, medieval and renaissance Cormòns come to life as the town hosts duels, games, and artisan markets in period costumes. The highlight is the Torneo Cavalleresco, a thrilling reconstruction of a medieval jousting tournament; www.cormons.info.

Jazz & Wine (August and October): Two great arts come together in summer and autumn concerts when international jazz stars meet some of the world's best wines. www.controtempo.org

Festa dell'Uva (September): A colourful parade in early September celebrates grapes and the harvest using decorative allegorical floats. Wines and traditional dishes are accompanied by a food market, with games for kids.

Uvaggio nel Mondo (October-November): Cormòns' Enoteca (see p. 101) organizes a series of tastings of Friuli Venezia Giulia's regional DOC wines, and assesses their success. www.uvaggionel-mondo.com

Dolegna del Collio

Festa di San Martino (November): A thanksgiving harvest festival both religious and pagan, and local prizegiving; www.comune.dolegnadelcollio.go.it

Farra d'Isonzo

Alpe Adria Chamber Music Seminars (July): Two weeks in July during which young musicians from both sides of the Adrian Alps compete in and study chamber music; www.farmusica.org.

Mossa

Musical Festival at Villa Codelli (August): A high-level cycle of operettas and classical musical concerts hosted by the historic villa and its agriturismo (see p. 105).

Gorizia

èStoria (May); Three days dedicated to Gorizia's history as a multi-cultural centre and stage of some of the 20th century's bloodiest battles. Debates, book presentations and films on Gorizia's past are accompanied by their culinary counterparts in the city's *piazze* and *palazzi*; www.comune.gorizia.it.

Premio Collio (June): The Premio Collio – or Collio Prize – is given each year in honour of the founding father of the Collio's Consorzio, Sigismondo Douglas Attems di Petzenstein. The international prize is divided into three categories: scientific research into viticulture (including collaborative projects between universities and Friuli's winemakers); journalism and communications (for material helping to promote the Collio); and – new to 2009 – the Collio Cinema Prize that will be given to a professional or student film work that best explores the Collio in its narrative; www.collio.it.

Seghizzi International Choral Competition (July): New works for a cappella choirs compete in Gorizia in a tradition that has its roots in the working men's choirs of the area; www.seghizzi.it.

World Folklore Festival (last weekend of August): A colourful celebration of international folk dancing, music and art includes the Danzerini di Lucinico, a folk-dancing group with Giorgio Grion (see p. 101).

Gusti di Frontiera (September-October): These delicious frontier flavours set up stands along the central streets and parks of Gorizia, with stalls and tastings of wine and food from eastern Europe and beyond. www.comune.gorizia.it

Gusti di Frontiera brings food from many regions to Gorizia

San Floriano del Collio

Likof (May): This spring thanksgiving festival celebrates local artisans and their crafts and the bounty of the year's harvests: the first cherries and newly completed wines, traditional foods and dishes. In times past, the Likof was used on important days in the life of a rural family: on the completion of a house or end of the *vendemmia*; www.likof.org.

San Lorenzo d'Isonzo

International junior baseball tournament (July); www.dragbears.it.

Trieste

Following pages: View from Russiz over the Collio towards the mountains of Slovenia

The city hosts an agricultural fair (in June), several important film festivals, and boating events as well as the International Celtic Festival, which celebrates all aspects of Celtic culture, including food; www.triesteturismo.net.

Chapter 1

From Gorizia to San Floriano del Collio

via Oslavia, Bucuje, Valerisce and Giasbana

The Collio is located in the province of Gorizia. This chapter begins with the city of Gorizia before moving north to Oslavia and San Floriano del Collio, then down to Bucuje and across to Valerisce and Giasbana.

Gorizia

This lovely small city, with its wide tree-lined avenues and mittel-European feel has long played a strategic role in the to-ing and fro-ing of people, products and wines between Italy and the Austro-Hungarian empire and, more recently, Italy, Yugoslavia and Slovenia. It was here that the customs houses could be found for goods travelling into Italy from the eastern countries. Gorizia is positioned where the rivers Isonzo and Vipacco meet. The arrival of the train line from Austria in the 19th century accellerated Gorizia's expansion into a commercial and touristic city, as its lovely period villas, parks and gardens attest.

In earlier times, it was cited in 1001 as being 'a villa known as Goriza in the Slavic language'. During the Middle Ages, Gorizia's feudal counts ruled over Europe's largest diocese and battled with Aquileia's patriarch; the castle that still presides over the city is from this period. They finally made peace in 1202. In 1500, on the death of Leonardo, the last count of Gorizia, the *contea* came under Hapsburg rule, where it was to remain almost uninterruptedly for several centuries, until 1918. In the 18th century, Gorizia was the scene of several bloody

Opposite: Gravner vines at Oslavia with Monte Sabotino behind

Gorizia's onion domes recollect its Austro-Hungarian past

peasant revolts. The First World War had devastating conse-
quences for the city and its province, which found themselves at
the centre of strategic fighting. Large parts of the bourgeois city
were destroyed by bombing.

Caught in yet another series of devastating battles in the
Second World War, this frontier town was divided in 1947 when
its eastern border was closed by the Iron Curtain; the new city
of Nova Gorica sprang up on the Yugoslavian side. Gorizia continued to be known as the Nice of the Austro-Hungarian
empire; its streets are said to have been planted with roses. Since
2004, when Slovenia entered the European Union, Gorizia's
mood has been less tense and now, with the definitive removal
of the final barriers, it feels open to multi-culturalism, as you
can hear from the several languages spoken by residents in
town: Italian, Friulano, Slovenian and, occasionally, German.
Gorizia's role in this new, expanded landscape is still being
defined, but I find it an attractive, manageable small city that
is fun to explore for its cafés, bookshops and colourful food
market.

Gorizia: a food-buying excursion

Gorizia market: woman slicing porcini mushrooms

I was introduced to Gorizia's lively food scene by Marje
Baudains, a longtime resident of the city. The **Central Market** is
in a restructured iron and glass building of 1927, with some
decoration that looks period; the pristine, clean-smelling fish-
mongers' hall is adjacent to it. Inside, the large main hall is
divided into three bays, one for flower stalls, the central one for
fruit and vegetables, and the one nearest Via Boccaccio for the
home-grown produce of the local *contadini*. These often elderly
people come in from the surrounding countryside to set up a
crate or two of whatever they've been able to pick that morning
in their (usually organic) gardens: misshapen but delicious
aubergines or cucumbers, windfall apples, fresh-laid eggs or
lettuces. I also spotted in the market a box of very fine, baby
leaves of mint, fennel, chives and other herbs marked *erbe per
frittata*. In this local speciality, the coarsely chopped aromatic
herbs are added to beaten eggs before being cooked in what is
the Italian version of an omelette. Easy to make and delicious
hot or cold.

Depending on the season, you can admire mushrooms and
chestnuts from the nearby woods, hand-picked cherries and
yellow plums, or vast pumpkins for making soup or for stuffing
the ever-popular, seasonal gnocchi. Inside the building there is
also a stall of a Puglian farm, Masseria Ferraioli, whose

Gorizia market

products are on sale there: sun-dried tomatoes, home-cured olives, salted capers and other Mediterranean delicacies.

As for the fish section, the speedy Guzzon brothers, with their shaved heads and courteous ways, do their own fishing at Grado as well as bringing in a wide array of the delicious Adriatic fish, crustaceans and molluscs you also find in the Rialto market in Venice: *cappesante* (scallops on the half shell), *seppie* (cuttlefish); *calamaretti* (squid), *polipo* (fresh octopus), *vongole veraci* (tiny clams for pasta sauces and antipasti), *branzino* (sea bass), *sfogi* (small sole)… an endless list of very fresh seafood which, cooked, is often accompanied in this area by white or sun-yellow polenta. The Market is on Corso Verdi at the corner with Via Boccaccio. Open Monday to Friday 07.30 to 15.00; Saturday and 07.30 to 18.00.

The Guzzon brothers
selling fish in the market

On Via Boccaccio, which runs along one side of the market building, a strip of interesting little shops includes **Sementi e Granaglie di Walter Gravner** (Via Boccaccio, 25), selling dried beans and other pulses, polenta, seeds, including blue poppy and *lino* (flax), for baking the local mittel-European cakes, hand-made brooms, vegetable and herb seeds in packets, raffia, bird seed etc. A few doors along, you'll find the **Rosticceria** with ready-made food to take away, for lunch or a picnic.

Close to that, the **Salumeria** features many local sausages, salami and hams, including Gorizian *prosciutto cotto nel pane* (whole ham baked in a pastry crust), when it's in season. On the same pavement, around the corner on Corso Verdi is an **Alimentari**, or grocery shop, selling the great D'Osvaldo *prosciutto* from Cormòns (see p127), fresh *vitello tonnato* for a good ready-made lunch, and *gnocchi con le susine* when they are in season. For sustenance mid-morning, stop for a glass of wine, or *bicière de vin*, in any of the bars or osterie in the streets around the marketplace, accompanied by a slice of prosciutto or wedge of cheese. That's a local tradition, and one that will sure-ly die hard. **Pasticceria Cidin** (Via Marconi Guglielmo, 6; tel 0481 32561), makes its own pastries, including strudels, cookies, Sacher Torte and other Austro-Hungarian delicacies. **Pasticceria Centrale** (Via Giuseppe Garibaldi, 4; tel 0481 530131) is one of the best-known pastry shops in the city as it was opened in 1940. It bakes all kinds of breads, pastries and cakes as well as the famous rolled yeast bread stuffed with nuts, raisins and candied fruits known as *la Gubana goriziane* that is sold in pretty boxes. Stop in for a drink with your cake. **QBK Bar** is across the streeet from the market, and a good place to go for a coffee while you're shopping (Corso Verdi, 51).

The cheese counter at
Mosetti's shop

Mosetti (Via Crispi, 6; 0481 82004) is Gorizia's most important specialist wine and food shop, or delicatessen. Run by the Mosetti brothers, Luca and Fulvio, this elegant small treasure trove opened in 2000. The Mosettis sell selected wines, local and hand-made cheeses plus lots of artisan products from around Italy: Collio wines, Carso olive oils, local honeys, serious chocolates, designer cookies, Piemontese sauces... and many more delicious items that also make great presents to take home. The young men's father left his job as a tailor to take over a food and wine shop in the town's outskirts when a cooperative's store was about to close down. After his death, in 1998, his sons decided to keep the shop going. 'When we first opened here, in the town centre, the Gorizians were not accustomed to our type of displays and selections; they assumed it meant our foods were more expensive, but they're not,' says Luca. 'Now we have a very loyal following.' In their tempting cheese counter I spotted a speckled cheese and asked Luca about it. 'That's called Frant, and it's made above Ovaro by Gortani Farm at Santa Maria La Longa, near Palmanova. The cheese is broken up and refermented with black pepper; it's delicious with hot polenta' (www.gortanifarm.it).

Brooms outside Sementi Gravner

Health food stores are quite rare in these parts, but Bioè (Via Trieste, 145; tel 0481 520855) is a large organic (*biologico* in Italian) supermarket that sells everything from muesli to cheeses to Austrian-style whole-grain breads. There are local fruits and vegetables too, as well as pastries, cookies, and other savoury snacks.

If it's a chocolate shop you're after, Sweet Chocolate (Via Garibaldi, 10; 0481 530677) has a scrumptious display of *cioccolatini* and bars, hand-made by Antonella Varotto. Some are based on local ingredients, such as Carso honey. Antonella is also working on a series of chocolate ice creams. The attractive little boutique is on the ground floor of Palazzo Unione, which rents furnished apartments for people wanting to stay in Gorizia. The whole complex belongs to Fabrizio Manganelli, whose wholesale chocolate factory, Sweet Spa, is one of Italy's most important. It specializes in chocolate eggs.

If, after all that shopping you're in the mood to sit and have a coffee, try Caffè Teatro which is popular with the young (Corso Italia, 1; tel 0481 280187), or the modern Café Haus, known for its aperitivo buffet displays; it also functions as a disco on Wednesday and Friday evenings (Corso Italia, 40; tel 0481 531182). For some delicious ice creams, Gelateria La Girandola has a great range of flavours, including assorted ices made from organic fruits (Corso Italia, 76; tel 0481 550058). Enoteca

Giardino dei Vizi (Piazza Sant'Antonio, 10; tel 0481 536430, 348 1037108) is situated under the portico of one of the city's prettiest palazzi, and is a fine spot for a glass of white or red and a slice of prosciutto.

Finally, some reading matter: if you collect cookbooks, Libreria Editrice Gorizia (LEG) has an interesting selection of local recipe books if you can muster enough Italian to read them. There are also lovely prints of the area and rare books to admire.

Where to eat in Gorizia

Restaurant
Alla Luna Trattoria

Via Oberdan, 13
TEL 0481 530374
CLOSED Sun
evening; Mon
PRICE €€

This is the most colourful of the local *osterie* in the vicinity of the market: every inch of the interior is covered with pictures, dried posies, spoons, jelly moulds, old photos and other assorted curios. The jolly waitresses are dressed in quaint country-girl's dresses from Slovenia. Squeeze into the ever-crowded bar for a glass of wine and slice of prosciutto or hand-made cheese before, during or after lunch or dinner. If you want a full meal, make sure to book ahead as this popular venue is always crammed, whatever the season. At the small tables a smattering of Slovenian and Friulano will help: the menu is hand-written and peppered with words in both. This is a great place to sample Gorizia's *prosciutto cotto nel pane* (ham baked in crust), or *frico croccante* (crisped melted cheese), or the delicious peppery Frant cheese, served here with Mamma Celestina's special apple sauce. Bleks, oddly-cut noodles, are ever a favourite, as are stuffed *gnocchi*, thick soups and *palacinka* (pancakes) filled with cabbage or other vegetables. Main courses include goulash, *cevapcici* sausages and sautéed salame, and desserts are a must, for the strudels, Gorizian Gubana 'bathed' in Slivovitz, or the menu's 'coccole' dessert surprise. An interesting wine list complements this satisfying range, as does the knowledge that the fairly priced menu is very good value.

Restaurant, wine bar
Majda

Via Duca d'Aosta, 71
TEL 0481 30871
CLOSED Sun; dinner
only Sat-Tues
PRICE €€€

Gorizia has a tradition of talented women cooks. Majda Cicigoj has been at their vanguard for forty years, preparing meals in what was once an 19th-century coaching inn. Majda herself seems ageless, her red hair elegantly swept high in a chignon, her white chef's jacket always impeccable. Yet she has spent decades in her restaurant's tiny kitchen, carrying on the multi-cultural traditions that unite in Gorizia: Slovenian, Italian,

*Majda Cicigoj and
her daughter*

Croatian, Austrian. With her lively daughter, Katjusa, Majda
has created a very personal environment to enjoy her authentic
home cooking.

The inn's courtyard has been turned into what looks like an
exotic bazaar: potted plants, hanging lights and candles decorate
the outside tables, with the wine bar on one side and the restaurant on the other. In the wine bar, which is open all evening for
pre- and post-dinner drinks, and for wine and snacks for those
who don't want a full meal, you sit on big cushions or a zebra-
pattern sofa in what always reminds me of a perfect location for
a happening. This informal, softly-lit salon is a favourite place
for winemakers, artists and locals of all ages to convene and
share a glass of Champagne, sparkling or still wines from
Katjusa's hand-chosen wine list, which draws from the Collio
and Friuli, Slovenia and Croatia before widening out to Italy,
France and beyond. There's always good music, and Majda
keeps everybody happy by regularly sending platters of delicious
snacks over from the kitchen: meatballs and prosciutto, cheese
rolls and pickled vegetables, in the Gorizian equivalent to tapas.

The cosy restaurant's décor is equally eclectic, with large
colourful modern pictures alongside bunches of dried flowers
and old-fashioned family photos. This is the place to sample
classic soul food like chestnut and porcini soup; polenta with
chiodini mushrooms and rosemary; cheese dumplings topped
with heady truffles; local pastas such as *slivoki* that are stuffed
with potatoes and chives and sauced with the juices of roast
beef and marjoram. Desserts are as good as they get: crusty
apple pies using local apples and hand-made pastry; Majda has

Slicing prosciutto di San Daniele

that rare gift, an unfailing palate, that invariably makes food that is delicious, well-balanced and comforting. Her menu changes as spontaneously as the seasons, and draws from the deep well of flavours and experience of generations of mothers and grandmothers. Paired with her daughter's wines and generous hospitality, you'll leave impatient to keep coming back for more.

Restaurant

Rosenbar

Via Duca d'Aosta, 96
TEL 0481 522700
CLOSED Sun, Mon
PRICE €€€€

I'm a big fan of this restaurant, with its pared-down, modern mittel-European feel and impressive stance on food and wine. Chef Michela Fabbro and her partner, Piero Loviscek, have created what amounts to a manifesto about how and where they source their ingredients.

*Autumn pumpkins
at the market*

'We made a decision years ago to work only with local foods, drawing from the best of what this *territorio* has to offer, and to use as many organic ingredients as possible,' says Piero. 'I get up early in the morning and go to Gorizia's market to buy directly from the *contadini* who bring whatever vegetables and fruits they have picked that day,' says Michela. 'That means my dishes are, by definition, seasonal and local.' The same goes for seafood, which forms the other mainstay of Michela's *cucina*. Most comes from the nearby Adriatic. This philosophy applies to the wines too, which are carefully selected to be natural and, whenever possible, organically made. 'We believe sustainability is a central issue now, in whatever kind of work is being done, and running a restaurant is no exception,' says Piero.

Michela has style of her own in the cooking too. 'Gorizia is a melting pot of cultures, and I love to be inspired by them,' she says. That may be, but her signature is for dishes that are decep-tively simple, clean to the palate, and light. The menu follows its sources and changes daily, depending on what Michela finds to inspire her. In late summer, fresh anchovies are marinated and served with a pure potato purée, cubed ripe tomatoes and mint. The famed *gambero rosso*, or red shrimp, comes piping hot, with a web of delicate fried leeks. A smooth chickpea soup is topped with a veil of filo pastry and rosemary-scented octopus. Sclopit, a wild bitter herb, comes stacked with white lasagnette and ricotta. These are sensual, sensitive pairings and go well with the clean, macerated wines of nearby San Floriano and Oslavia. 'We're against the globalization and dumbing-down of foods and wines,' she explains. 'Having a palate for fresh, uncluttered tastes is something we can all develop. My very aged father can still recognize good ingredients when he tastes them, and rejects any that are not. He's set a good example for us.' Michela too is setting a good example, one that has been recognized by Slow Food, who selected her to be amongst its 1,000 chefs supporting sustainability at Terra Madre.

Wine Bar, Hotel, Restaurant
Grand Hotel Entourage

Piazza San Antonio, 2
TEL 0481 550235
www.entouragegorizia
.com

Brilliantly located in the centre of town, this 4-star hotel is in the elegant Palazzo Strassoldo, and offers rooms in a variety of prices, from B&B to luxurious suites. In addition to its restau-rant, Il Bearnese, the Entourage is known for its well-stocked wine bar, Il Vinattiere Di Chambord, where the best of the Collio wines are always available, accompanied by tasty snacks from selected cheeses to imaginative crostini.

Detail from a Gorizia villa façade

GORIZIA: GARDENS, PALAZZI AND CULTURE

There are several interesting gardens and palazzi in and around Gorizia, many begun in the 19th century when visitors from northern parts of the Austro-Hungarian empire marvelled at the beauty of Gorizia's horticulture. These are still open to the public at various times throughout the year.

The tree-lined Giardini Pubblici are in Piazza Cesare Battisti, and are open all year, as are the Parco del Municipio and Parco della Rimembranza. Villa Ritter's garden is currently being revamped around its centenarian trees.

Parco di Villa Coronini is open to the public and was donated to the city by the Fondazione Palazzo Coronini Cronberg. It's a real *giardino all'italiana*, with statues, architectural set pieces and ancient trees. Visits are also recommended to the marvellous historic 16th-century Palazzo Coronini Cronberg (Viale XX Settembre, 14; tel 0481 533485; www.coronini.it), now one of the most fascinating museums in the area for its portrayal of noble life.

Luciano Viatori's magnificent private botanical garden is an ever-changing tribute to the passions of its creator. The vast floral park is located on the hillside of Piuma, just outside the city of Gorizia. Spread over 2.5 hectares of sloping ground, it now houses a unique collection of rhododendrons, azaleas, over 200 magnolias, and an infinite amount of other flowering plants. Viatori has spent over 17 years making the garden, and opens it to the public during the flowering season on Sunday afternoons after 16.00 from early spring through early summer. Tel 0481 32636.

The Fondazione Cassa di Risparmio di Gorizia is a culturally influential foundation linked to a savings bank begun in the 1830s. Active in the arts, conservation, schools and charities, to name but a few of its interests, the Fondazione owns many valuable collections, including those on display in the Musei Provinciali di Palazzo Attems, in Piazza De Amicis, 2, Gorizia. www.fondazionecarigo.it.

The well restored Castello high above Gorizia's town centre now houses a medieval museum.

For more information: www.comune.gorizia.it, www.provincia.gorizia.it, or www.isontino.com.

Opposite: A woodland walk in the magnificent Viatori garden in spring

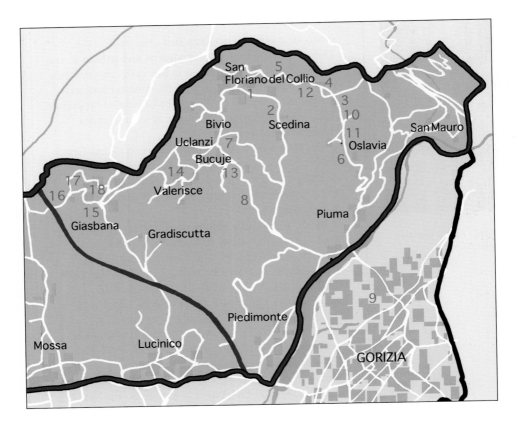

Oslavia and San Floriano del Collio

On a clear day you can see the sea from the piazza of San Floriano, the highest point of the Collio, at 276 metres. It's also the closest part of the Collio to the water, and benefits from the warm sea breezes carried on the winds from Trieste. Despite its altitude, San Floriano has a longer season than other parts of the Collio, with as much as two to three extra weeks of growing time for the locals' vegetable gardens. San Floriano also has a very steep terrain, and it's particularly hard here to work the vineyard terraces with a tractor: one producer told me he spent more time carefully turning his small tractor on the slopes than working the rows! All those extra hours of labour mean that prices must necessarily be higher here than in the plain where so much more is now mechanized.

The area in and around San Floriano, including Oslavia and Lucinico, were completely devastated during the World Wars, as the monolithic Oslavia ossuary – built in 1938 – attests. It contains the bones of 57,000 soldiers killed during the Great War, of whom 36,000 were unknown. Not only were the hills here completely riddled with trenches, some of which are still being uncovered almost 90 years later, but they were bare of all trees. What trees existed around the pastures were either cut down for fortifications or else destroyed by the bombings. After the Second World War, nature was encouraged to return: Evangelos Paraschos told me there are now more woods in San Floriano than when it was under Austrian rule.

Although San Floriano has a mere 800 inhabitants, the township boasts 27 kilometres of roads. From a winemaking perspective, San Floriano and Oslavia are known for the quality of their grapes, as well as the radical winemaking movements that originated here over the last 30 years. In particular, San Floriano is known for its Ribolla Gialla.

San Floriano del Collio

Restaurant
Dvor Trattoria

Via Castello, 5
TEL 0481 884035
CLOSED Monday;
Thursday
PRICE €€

Located at the big curve in the road that leads up to San Floriano from Valerisce, Dvor is a classic osteria serving unfussy, down-to-earth food at fair prices. It's a nice place for a summer's lunch or dinner, when it's hot and sticky in the plain. 'Dvor' means 'courtyard' in Slovenian, and here, in the large enclosed garden with fabulous views of the whole landscape, you can sit out under the chestnut trees at simple wooden tables. There are rustic pastas; meats are cooked simply, *alla*

The view across the
valley at Uclanzi

brace, over wood embers, and include the thin, spiced Slovenian
sausages, *cevapcici*, that are served with a red-pepper sauce.
Dessert invariably include a strudel. Wines are strictly local, a
small list with a few nice choices.

Restaurant

Korsic Osteria

Kraj Sovenza, 7
TEL 0481 884248
CLOSED Tuesday;
Wednesday
PRICE €€€

This osteria sits at the T-junction connecting the San
Floriano/Oslavia to Slovenia road, and the road that leads
towards the Collio and Valerisce. On a warm summer's day sit
outside in the garden at rustic wooden tables; in cooler weather
eat indoors in the large, luminous modern dining room that
overlooks the garden. Popular for the ample outdoor grill that
offers all sorts of meats, Korsic also prepares traditional fare
and some more adventurous dishes. Try the local *biechi* (rough-
cut egg noodles) or seasonal *gnocchi* (pumpkin-flavoured in

autumn, topped with toasted sunflower seeds). The young chef likes working with local, well-flavoured ingredients: bitter radicchio, home-cured pork, polenta, hand-made and smoked cheeses, and often combines several of them in a single dish. The desserts are hearty too: *palacinka* (stuffed Slovenian crêpes) or fried *snita* (Slovenian eggy-bread) served with fruit cream, or home-baked cakes. A strictly local wine list accompanies the food. There's a little bar near the entrance if you prefer just stopping for a coffee, drink or snack.

Restaurant
Vogric Trattoria

Uclanzi, 23
TEL 0481 884095
CLOSED Tues-Weds
PRICE €€

On the high road that curves between San Floriano and Valerisce, this is a big, busy, affordable place that local families enjoy for a Sunday lunch outing with the kids. If you don't mind the well-organized hustle and bustle and the cafeteria style food, go for grilled meats, generous portions of pasta and the jolly atmosphere.

Oslavia and San Floriano del Collio wineries

Wine
Conti Formentini

Via Oslavia
San Floriano del Collio
TEL 0481 884131
www.giv.it

Conti Formentini is one of the oldest of the historic Collio estates, with cellars located right in the village centre of San Floriano. The Formentini family originally bought the 14th-century castle in 1512. The modern winery was founded in the 1960s, and was among the first in the area to bottle its wines. At that time most of the vineyards were owned by three families; Formentini bought out the other two and was left with one of the largest single blocks of vineyards in the Collio. Today, the Formentini family still own the castle and run a restaurant, hotel and golf club on the grounds, Golf Hotel Castello Formentini. Michele Formentini, a lawyer, also has an exceptional collection of old winemaking tools that are on display in a museum dedicated to rural culture, or *civiltà contadina*, at Aiello del Friuli.

The Collio Consortium's distinctive blue sign at Conti Formentini

Gruppo Italiano Vini (GIV) is the leading Italian wine group, with headquarters in Verona. It has over 14 important estates throughout Italy under its wing, from Sicily to Piedmont and Friuli. In 1994, GIV bought the Conti Formentini winery. I asked GIV's managing director, Emilio Pedron, why? 'Conti Formentini is one of the Collio's most prestigious names. We have always believed in the Collio as the place with the best vocation for making white wines in Italy,' he says. 'Rather like a white Montalcino. That's the positive aspect. The sadder truth is that too much of the Collio's wine is sold simply as Pinot Grigio. There's nothing wrong with that grape variety, but Pinot Grigio doesn't need the Collio to be sold. I am now convinced that the way forward for us in the Collio is to concentrate on the native grape varieties and on the Collio Bianco blend. That way we can focus on the specific qualities the Collio brings to its wines that justify its 'niche' status.' Recent decisions taken at the winery plan to drastically reduce the portfolio of wines being made there, put Ribolla Gialla, Sauvignon, and Friulano in the spotlight, and gradually phase reds out altogether. 'GIV can offer its customers a wide range of great reds from many other areas of Italy, but we may maintain some Cabernet Franc as that works particularly well in the Collio,' says Pedron. GIV's market for its Collio whites is primarily within Italy at the moment, due to its earlier decision to produce large quantities of Pinot Grigio. 'Italians immediately recognize that a wine made in the Collio – including Pinot Grigio – has an extra gear, *una marcia in più*, and they are willing to pay more for it.' Pedron is resisting the call for ever more Pinot Grigio and hopes the new strategy will make a series of unique wines from indigenous grapes that will be recognized for their superior value beyond Italy's shores.

Sauvignon Blanc grapes

When I visited the estate it was harvest time, and Marco del Piccolo showed me around. He is the resident winemaker and began working for the winery when it was owned by the Formentini family. He explained that GIV owns no vineyards but, as a cooperative, vinifies the grapes grown by around 30 of the co-op's members from 80 hectares of vineyards. Most are in San Floriano and Oslavia, the Collio's highest territory. 'When GIV came in they immediately invested in modernizing the cellar here,' explains del Piccolo as he shows me the extensive vinification and underground ageing rooms on two floors. There are three large VIM presses, and rows of neat barriques. Del Piccolo is keen to work with other local and traditional woods, acacia and chestnut. He is trying to phase out weed-killers and experimenting varying lengths of maceration for the grapes, most of which are processed at controlled, cold temperatures to retain their freshness. At present, the winery is producing circa 550,000 bottles, with two lines of wines, including the selected Conti Formentini line. This includes a 'ramato', or copper-coloured, Pinot Grigio, and Rylint, named after the 16th-century abbess, Rylint Formentini. This is a crisp Collio Bianco DOC blend of Chardonnay, Pinot Grigio and Sauvignon vinified in steel.

Wine

Draga

Scedina, 8
San Floriano del Collio
TEL 0481 884182
www.draga.it

The Miklus family have their home and winery in one of the most beautiful of the Collio's valleys, below San Floriano at Scedina. From here, at Draga, the views are spectacular, looking out across vineyards towards Slovenia, the Oslavia monument and Gorizia, or else back across the Italian Collio towards Monte Calvario. If you arrive at the house when the family is in the vineyards or cellars, their dog Tex will alert them of your visit, with one bark for friends and another for strangers.

Milan and his wife, Anna, have ten hectares of vineyards, in two large pieces, which in itself is unusual here, as so many San Floriano vineyards are much smaller than that. Of these, one contains a plot of 50-year-old Tocai vines. Milan and his sons, Mitja and Dennis, do all the work themselves, tying the vines onto their supports by hand using willow shoots, here called *vimini*. Unlike most modern producers, Milan decided not to radically change the traditional trellis system, the *cappuccina*, in one of the vineyards in which the vines are trained high. 'I was put under pressure to make the change and cut the vines way down, but I resisted, and I'm glad I did,' the good-natured Milan says. 'The Ribolla Gialla likes to get a lot of sun, and needs the purest *ponca* soil to do well, which we have here,' he adds. The Ribolla is given a 15-day maceration on the skins, with the cap being punched down manually every six to seven hours. I visited when the Ribolla grapes had been in the open-

Above: Milan Miklus tastes a grape to decide if it's harvest time

*Anna and Milan Miklus
with their sons Mitja and
Dennis*

*The view towards
Oslavia from a Draga
vineyard, with table
ready for the harvesters*

topped tank for just a week, and I was keen to try my hand at this *follatura*. The men all stood around and watched, amused but pleased with my efforts: it's hard work pushing the thick layer of grapes back down under the must, using a long wooden tool that looks like a broom without the bristles. After fermentation, the Ribolla goes half into large wooden barrels and half into stainless steel tanks, to be assembled later; it comes out within one year. Aside from the reds, the Miklus also make a Collio Bianco blend of assorted white wines, Bianco di Collina: Chardonnay, Riesling and Sauvignon, with a little Tocai added – the proportions change yearly.

The family has built its cellar by hand too, bit by bit, embellishing it with architectural elements they've found at the flea markets to give it a personal character. 'In the old days the local families here would all help each other with the seasonal cherry picking or vine pruning, and the women would bring baskets of bread for lunch, but that spirit has changed and now it's pretty much each to himself,' says Milan a little regretfully. The Miklus' spirit of hospitality lives on, however. Milan has built two beautiful big tables under the trees by the vineyards to host the harvest lunches, and there's never a shortage of home-made *salame* or cheese to accompany a glass of fine wine at their house.

Via Lenzuolo Bianco, 1
Oslavia
TEL 0481 547103
www.fieglvini.com

Wine
Fiegl

Martin Fiegl is one of the new generation of winemakers in the Collio. In his mid twenties, he's already been made vice-president of the Consortium, and plays an active role in promoting the area and its wines. His family's estate is on the crest of the hill at Oslavia that looks out towards Monte Sabotino, the forest-covered mountain that forms Nova Gorica's protective shoulder. 'Before Slovenia came into the EU, the road that crosses that mountainside was completely sealed off: it goes from Slovenia to Nova Gorica via Italy but when you took it you weren't allowed out into Italy,' he says, pointing across a valley of vineyards to a diagonal road cutting through the woods. Recently, Martin and a couple of his Italian winemaking friends, Kristian Keber and Stefano Bensa, teamed up with three young wine producers from Slovenia to make the world's first transborder wine, of grapes from both sides. 'Our idea with Vinolimes is to push the bureaucrats from the two countries to create a joint IGT which would reunite what was, for centuries, a single wine-making *territorio*. Not only would it be a first step in bringing unity to this divided land, but it would also reflect well on both the Collio and Slovenian (Brda) consortia.'

The generational change is not just a matter of taking over the pruning work in the vineyards from a father or uncle. 'Some of my peers are already travelling the world to sell their wines. I feel we're sitting on a gold mine. We've seen the value of what the Collio has to offer, and are energized about communicating it, but many others are still too tied to traditional roles here,' he says.

Records show that the Fiegl family has been in Oslavia since 1782, as seen on the Austrian land register. 'My father, Giuseppe, and his brothers, Alessio and Rinaldo, ran the farm and in 1992 they started bottling their own wines, instead of selling the grapes as they had before. I wish they had begun sooner,' says Martin. The estate has grown since then, from twenty hectares of vineyards to thirty, and now produces 150,000 bottles, of which 80% are white wines. 'We're a medium-sized family winery, as most of the small ones in the Collio have circa five hectares,' he says. Martin's mother, Silvana, greets visitors and leads tastings and tours of the new cellars, complete with the collection of war memorabilia the Fiegls have found in the vineyards. Most of the estate's single-varietal whites are worked in steel; the Collio Bianco blend, Leopold, is a mix of Friulano, Pinot Bianco, Sauvignon and Ribolla Gialla, aged in part in barriques for eight months.

Martin Fiegl

Wine

Gravner

Via Lenzuolo Bianco, 9
Oslavia
TEL 0481 30882
www.gravner.it

Some rooms are unlike any other spaces you've ever entered. The room I have in mind is far from public view, a work room with no embellishments and barely any lighting. A dirt floor. Yet it takes my breath away each time I go there. It's the room where Josko Gravner has the amphoræ he uses to vinify his wines. When you go down the stairs into this cellar all you see are the round necks of man-sized clay jars protruding from the ground like the circular tips of many icebergs whose large bellies are buried in the earth below them, filled with wine. Whether it's those bodies of fermenting wine or the tension in the clay of such extraordinary vessels that give the room its unusual energy, I'm not sure. But energy it has. (The first time I saw it I was reminded of the scene in Eisenstein's film, *Strike*, in which a group of people emerge, Bosch-like, from a field full of giant buried urns.)

Josko Gravner

'The amphoræ come from Georgia, in the Caucasus, where they are still being made by hand and used for winemaking,' says Miha, Josko's son, who now runs the 18-hectare estate with his father and mother, Maria. 'Inside, they are sealed with beeswax. Once a year, after they've been emptied of their wine, I lower myself down inside to clean them: I have to stay thin enough to fit!' At harvest time, each jar is filled with very ripe, healthy grape berries.

'This is a pre-Roman method,' Josko Gravner explains. 'Archæologists have discovered that in the beginnings of wine-making, in Iraq and Babylonia, figs were used to trigger the fermentation. The amphoræ are the oldest model we have. In Georgia they are buried outdoors, which allows the wines to follow the full cycle of the seasons.'

I was fascinated to learn how such an archetypal system of winemaking works. For the first weeks, the white or red grapes are left to macerate in the open-topped amphoræ as the fermentation gets under way using wild yeasts. The skins rise to the top and form a thick layer which is manually pushed down into the must five times a day at first, gradually reducing to once a day. After the malolactic fermentation has run its course, in December the jars are topped up and sealed with granite covers until the following April. 'During this period, the residues (*vinacce*) settle in the amphoræ's pointed bottom; the wine is pumped off, the *vinacce* are pressed in a 1950's press and the wine returned to the amphoræ, minus the lees. The wines remain there until autumn, when they are transferred to large wooden barrels.' The wines then age in wood for several years

Opposite: Gravner's amphora cellar

*Two disused amphoræ
in a Gravner vineyard
at Oslavia*

before being bottled, bottle-fined, and sold. No filtering, and
only a tiny pinch of sulphites when the grapes go into the
amphoræ and when bottling. Josko Gravner has been a catalyst
and role model for some of the Collio's winemakers, and a
controversial figure to others. He has gone through many
successful phases, or chapters, of winemaking before commit-
ting himself to this one: from using cement tanks, steel tanks
and cold temperatures for his whites, to fermenting and ageing
them in barriques, which he was instrumental in introducing
into Friuli in the 1980s. 'In the end, I've chosen to make wines
as naturally as possible,' he says. 'And eliminated everything
that is inessential: fridges, stainless-steel tanks, filters, clari-
fiers... I don't even analyze the grapes any more. It's enough to
taste them to know when to harvest. Wine is like a sponge that
absorbs the thoughts of the person making it. Using all that
technology you lose the poetry of winemaking.'

If this appears homespun or bucolic, don't be fooled. Not
only does Gravner have an exceptional and experienced palate,
but the use of the amphoræ and the ability to leave the grapes
almost to their own devices once they are in the cellar necessi-
tate the most exacting work in the vineyards. 'The amphoræ are
like big speakers: they amplify whatever is in the wine, be it
good or bad,' Josko explains.

The Gravner vineyards are some of the most perfect I've seen –
outside of France. The Gravners don't consider themselves
organic or bio-dynamic. 'We try to do as little damage to nature

as possible,' says Miha. 'What's the point of being certified organic and then chilling the must technologically: that's a contradiction in terms.' They have a tractor and spray the vines six times yearly with copper and sulphur, and use potassium sulphate. 'We haven't used any systemic treatments for over ten years and our vines are extremely strong and healthy. Once the vines are aged ten years or more, the vineyards are under-planted with grasses. 'Our aim is to maintain our vines for as long as we can: 50, 60, even 80 years.' Grape production is kept to a minimum to concentrate each plant's energy into just two or three bunches. Walk through the vineyards right up until harvest time, which in their case is in late September and October, and you'll see the ground littered with the 50 percent of bunches they have cut away.

In the case of Ribolla Gialla, the native grape that Gravner has been instumental in relaunching, the bunches are also cut in half to make them smaller. 'We look for botrytis, or 'noble rot' to set in to help bring sweetness to our Ribolla, and that only happens when the plant's production is very low,' says Miha. 'We also follow the moon's cycle for all the important work, from pruning to the annual racking,' says Josko.

In another courageous, if not radical move, Gravner has decided to reduce his grape varieties to just two over the next ten years: Ribolla Gialla and the red, Pignolo. This will eliminate the varieties that currently go into his award-winning Breg, including Pinot Grigio, Chardonnay and Sauvignon. Indeed, he'll stop making it. 'Ribolla Gialla has been planted here in Oslavia and on the Slovenian side of the Collio hills for over a thousand years, and it's better than any of the other grape varieties, including Tocai and Malvasia,' says Josko. 'Ribolla is also the white grape best suited to the long macerations which can increase the complexity, minerality and structure of the wines. As for Pignolo, it was abandoned in our area because it's hard to grow and to prune, but it's giving us real satisfaction when we wait long enough.' The Gravner Pignolo comes out ten years after the harvest. 'You need that much time if you are not using modern technology to soften its tannins.'

Miha Gravner

In 2008, I was lucky to taste the 2003 Ribolla Gialla Riserva from the barrel; it was made from very old vines that were about to be grubbed up. A clear, soft amber colour, the wine's complex bouquet of herbal notes, with hints of pine resin and eucalyptus, complemented its sweet fruit aromas of apricots and grapes; in the mouth, the fruit is joined by toasty, salted caramel and a mineral energy that unfolds into the long, dynamic finale. A unique, inspiring, unforgettable wine.

Wine

Il Carpino

Sovenza, 14a
San Floriano del Collio
TEL 0481 884097
www.ilcarpino.com

Franco and Anna Sosol's cellar is in an enviable position: it's perched like an eyrie on the side of a high hill, just off the road that winds down from San Floriano towards Oslavia, and commands wide views of Monte Sabotino across the steep valley. This is the frontier with Slovenia and eastern Europe, the north-easternmost part of Italy. Here the vineyards are fortunate to be surrounded by woods and constant currents of air which help keep the grapes aerated and disease free. The couple set up the winery in 1987, with the help of Anna's late father, Silvano, and have recently happily been joined in the business by their children, Naike, who studied languages and Manuel, who trained as a cook. Both daughter and son are now learning each stage of the winemaking process, from pruning to pairing wine to food.

'When we began,' says Franco, 'we were helped by the talented winemaker, Roberto Cipresso, a good friend even if he's no longer our consultant. He encouraged us to plant at high densities and to reduce the vines' output. That's a philosophy we've stuck to.' In particular, native Ribolla Gialla must be kept below 1 kilo of fruit per plant for the grapes to ripen fully. The Sosols prefer natural selected yeasts to the chemical brands that are now prevalent.

Franco adds that he likes to work the vineyards much as the 'vecchi' did, the older generation who carved out the terraces and tilled the land by hand. 'We're not completely organic, but we like to keep chemical interference to a minimum,' he says, 'and our high position here certainly helps us in that.'

Once the grapes are brought into the cellar, they go to produce two distinct lines of wines: Vigna Runc, which are white and red wines made exclusively from young vines and worked in stainless steel to keep them fresh and drinkable; and the Carpino line. Here the Sosols bring together the best grapes of the 15-hectare estate. 'Up until three years ago we vinified all our grapes in bianco, using cold temperatures, but recently we've adopted a different strategy and are much happier with the results.' Here the grapes undergo macerations of four or more days, and the wines are worked in barrels, with French barriques now giving way to large Slavonian oak barrels that allow the fruit to be more expressive. Of these, I was impressed by Exordium, made from aged Tocai Friulano vines. The grapes are macerated for six days and fermentation takes place on the skins; the wine spends twelve months in tonneaux. The result is a pure, elegant wine with a razor-sharp mineral nerve. Vis Uvae or 'the force of the grapes' is a copper-toned Pinot Grigio that

The view from San Floriano towards Oslavia and Monte Sabotino

spends almost a week macerating on the skins before being aged in large barrels and bottled, unfiltered. These wines are allowed plenty of time to evolve in the bottle, and are released usually after more than two years.

Wine

La Castellada

Oslavia, 1
Gorizia
TEL 0481 33670
nicolobensa@virgilio.it

La Castellada is a real country farmhouse positioned in the midst of Oslavia, one of the Collio's most important crus. It's surrounded by vineyards and overlooks the valley from a wonderfully open, high position. This pioneering estate was founded by the brothers Bensa, Giorgio and Nicolò; with Nico's wife Valentina and their sons Stefano and Matteo.

'When we moved here, in 1980, the hill had been abandoned by the *contadini* who had left the country for work in the cities,' explains Nico as he shows me the vineyards nearest the house. 'Starting out as young people in 1985, we were fascinated by change and modernity. We had little faith in tradition. Like Gravner and Radikon, we experimented with everything: thirty-five years ago we used large barrels, then we went to cement, to steel, to French barriques, and back to large barrels again. I'm not sure that whole winemaking "journey" was worth it, but each step felt right at the time.' In what Bensa describes as the opposite of a modern approach, they don't use selected yeasts

Nicolò Bensa and
his family

La Castellada vineyards
on a steep hill at Oslavia

and have reduced the use of sulphites to a minimum – often avoiding them altogether. 'I've noticed that this way the wines taste much more of fruit,' he says.

White grapes are macerated on the skins for six to eight days (longer for the Ribolla) and allowed to ferment in open-topped conical barrels to encourage wild yeasts. Then they are aged in the traditional way, in large wooden barrels that allow the wine to breathe without imparting vanilla flavours, often for more than one year. La Castellada produces four whites and one red. Bensa also follows the moon's cycles to determine when to inter-act with the wines. 'There's an old saying here: he who watches the moon may end up in the ditch!' he laughs. 'Well, I watch it but not in a fanatical way. Our grandparents followed the moon's cycles and it's true that when the moon is old, that's the moment of maximum stability for the wines: you can rack them then and the deposit stays firmly rooted to the bottom of the barrel.' La Castellada's wines are rich, mineral and unfiltered; here again, the moon's cycle helps them bottle as little sediment as possible. Today, the Bensas are devoting ever more time to the vineyards and have been studying which plants have the most perfumed grapes and can best withstand disease. 'What I'd really like to do,' says Nico, 'is return to the way the *contadini* lived long ago, in the sense of being self-sufficient. That old-fashioned way to live seems ever more modern to me.'

Wine
Muzic

Bivio, 4
San Floriano del Collio
TEL 0481 884201
www.cantinamuzic.it

The Muzic family's house and cellar command breathtaking views over vineyards towards Nova Gorica, Gorizia and the mountains of the Carso. Orieta and her husband, whose name is

Giovanni but who is known as Ivan, have thirteen hectares of vines in the Collio and two in Isonzo. They're on the top of a natural amphitheatre at 200 metres above sea level in a sheltered microclimate that allows even prickly pears to grow. The cellar's courtyard is filled with objects they've uncovered in their vineyards: fragments from both World Wars, from pieces of shell to metal helmets and drinking cans. It's an all too vivid reminder of this borderland's history.

'We're on the border in more ways than one,' explains Ivan. 'In the 1950s, under Italian law, babies born in this area had to be christened with Italian names even though we all spoke Slovenian at home and at school.'

'Ours is the oldest remaining *cantina* in San Floriano,' says Orieta as we walk below the house, past stainless steel vinification tanks to a small cellar with red-brick vaulting in the ceiling and stone walls that probably date to 1750. 'It's hard to believe, but after the First World War only four of the 240 houses in the village were left standing.'

The Muzic house was rebuilt in 1927; Ivan's parents lived there and rented land from a landowner in Piedimonte, near Gorizia. In 1962 they were able to buy their first five hectares. 'At that time there were peach and cherry orchards here, and cows in the barn,' says Ivan. Like many *contadini*, Ivan's father

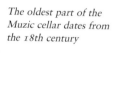

The oldest part of the Muzic cellar dates from the 18th century

Vineyards below the
Muzic cellar

sold grapes in the early seventies to the Cantina Produttori of
Cormòns, a cooperative to which he belonged. Later, he began
selling wine in large tanks to wholesalers, and *sfuso* to the public. 'We finally started bottling our own wine in 1990,' he continues, 'just before the big grape-price crisis that affected so
many small growers here.' The Muzics are often advised by
their friend, winemaker Giorgio Bertossi, who comes to taste
and exchange ideas with them.

Both of the Muzic's sons, Elija and Fabijan, have studied at
Cividale's school of enology and now take an active part in the
family business. 'It's great for us,' says Orieta, 'because our family dinner conversation in the kitchen is usually about wine. Our
sons are very enthusiastic and are already experimenting with
new ideas in the vineyards and the cellar.'

The family produce a range of wines from some very well-
located vineyards in and around San Floriano, including vineyards with wonderful old vines. This includes a series of mono-
varietal wines as well as a Collio white blend, Bric. This is a
blend of Tocai Friulano, Malvasia Istriana and Ribolla Gialla,
the three grapes native to the area. This wine is allowed to
remain for several months on the lees in oak barrels. 'We in the
Collio may not be able to compete with New World pricing,'
says Ivan, 'but they can't compete with what we have here: lots
of passionate small producers, each with his or her own ideas
and very personal wines made from these great terroirs. That's a
unique situation.'

Wine

Bucuje, 13a
San Floriano del Collio
TEL 0481 884154
www.paraschos.it

Paraschos

You have to be Italian to get the visual pun in Paraschos' bold wine labelling. Evangelos Paraschos is Greek. In Italian, the symbol for 'pi' is called 'P Greco' – 'Greek P'. So his bottles tip you off to their maker's nationality. Greek P – π + not = Pinot, and you've got the grape type. Whatever's written on the bottles, the colour of their contents would tip you off to Paraschos' winemaking style, as he is making macerated wines from grapes grown in vineyards without using chemicals.

Paraschos has been living in Italy for more years than he can remember, about thirty. He's been making wine though for ten years, from vines he bought in 1997. Today, he owns 5.5 hectares and has another 4.5 on a long lease; he works them as if they were his own. Most of these vineyards are between San Floriano, Oslavia and Lucinico, with one hectare just over the border in Slovenia. Evangelos is helped in the winemaking by his son, Alexis. Before making wines, he worked with his wife Nadja in the restaurant her family used to run. She is a fantastic cook, and makes the best *gnocchi di susine* – potato dumplings stuffed with plums – I've tasted (see p. 14 for a photograph).

'My idea is to go back to the way vines used to be grown, as our great-grandfathers did, without weedkillers or chemical fertilizers,' says Paraschos. When it's needed, I only use well-rotted manure. We cut the grass in the vineyards by hand after letting it go to seed. Grass in the vineyards has a function: it absorbs humidity when it rains, and it also gives back important elements. I'm less convinced that nitrogen (*azoto*) is needed, but I do think that carbon (*carbonio*) is a very important element, one you can only get from grass. Grasses need to complete their

Evangelos Paraschos and his son Alexis

life cycles too, which is why we cut after they have gone to seed, not before.' The only product Paraschos uses for spraying the vines against disease is the classic 'Bordeaux' mixture of copper and sulphur. This leaves the vines vulnerable to attack, as in the difficult spring of 2008, but it's a risk he's prepared to take.

In the cellar, 'technology only serves where it's useful,' he says. The white grapes are destalked and crushed lightly before being put into large open-topped vats for fermentation, as if they were red grapes. No selected yeasts are used, as Paraschos prefers wild yeasts. The cap is punched down every three hours while the must is fermenting. Since Paraschos uses no sulphites, he has to be careful not to let the wines oxidize after fermentation. 'Macerating times vary by grape type, he says, 'but the minimum is seven days as it's important to extract the antioxidants in the grape skins.' Then the must is pressed and left for two days to decant naturally before being run off into large oval barrels for ageing, or into conical barrels to finish fermentation, with bâtonnages until Christmas. The wine will remain on the lees in the barrels for two years. Temperatures in the cellar are naturally controlled by opening and closing the windows. The whites remain in bottles for several months before being sold; wines made from old vines may spend four years in the barrel before being bottled, barrels with light or no toasting being favoured. Paraschos does not filter his wines so as not to lose any of these anti-oxidants; he racks during the waning moon.

Paraschos doesn't hesitate to credit Gravner and Radikon with being the pioneers in this field of winemaking. 'It's not only for the maceration that we owe them our thanks, but especially for their work in the vineyards: it's the idea that you could work white grapes differently on the vine in order to produce great wines that has inspired us.'

Paraschos' Pinot Grigio, is vinified on the skins. It's a soft salmon-caramel colour, with exotic notes of rhubarb, wild thyme and dried mint to the nose, and very fine, long energy in the mouth. His Tocai, (Greek T + kai, τ + και), has a more floral nose, hinting at muscat and tea leaves, with a grassy note that recurs in his wines. Paraschos sees reds as more masculine and rough, whites more feminine and mellow. 'I think you need to approach this kind of white wine differently from other whites, more like an old red, and not be burdened with preconceptions about colour or taste. Try them with food, served no cooler than 14°C, and you'll be amazed how well they go.'

At the entrance to Paraschos' cellar and tasting room are some beautiful Greek terracotta urns. 'These are hand-made,

The invaiatura, *when the grapes change colour*

but just for decoration. The original Greek amphoræ were pointed at one end, but were never used buried in the ground.'

Wine

Damijan Podversic

Via Brigata Pavia, 61
Gorizia
TEL 0481 78217
damijan.go@virgilio.it
www.damijanpodversic.
com

The *vendemmia*, or harvest, is over for some and has not yet begun for others. It's early October and if most of the Collio's grapes are safely in their vinification vats or barrels, Damijan Podversic is blissfully untroubled. He's waiting it out. 'We've been lucky this year with a long period of sun and warmth in autumn that will help our grapes not only ripen fully but, in the case of Ribolla Gialla, also hopefully bring on botrytis – the so-called 'noble rot' – that concentrates its sugars,' says Damijan, as we take a tour of his vineyards. These are located on the slopes of Monte Calvario, scene of some of the most bloody battles in the First World War. Damijan has reclaimed parts of these vineyards from the woods that had over-run them, rebuilding the old terraces that were a legacy of the area's viticultural heritage, ninety years ago. Damijan is a big, strapping young man with very clear ideas about his work.

'You can't be a little producer and think like a big one: to make it as an independent you have to have a strong philosophy behind your winemaking, one that represents your way of life, not just your business,' he says. Like his mentor, Josko Gravner, Damijan Podversic has made a commitment to natural winemaking.

'I was lucky enough to meet Gravner in 1985. I was so impressed by him that I returned to see him again the next day. And every day after that until he agreed to take me on as a sort of apprentice. I was very young at the time. I had bought my first little vineyards at eighteen. I was determined that I wanted to work on the land, as my grandfather had. At first my father was for it, but when I began to follow Gravner in his thinking,

my father turned against me. It's easy now to forget how un-
popular Gravner was at that time: hardly anyone understood
the choices he was making about macerating and, later,
the amphoræ.'

Fortunately, Damijan had the support of his wife, Elena, with
whom he has three children. 'Just three things matter to me: my
vineyards, my family, and my wine,' he says. Damijan is respect-
ful of both soil and plants in his vineyards. 'People should take
the trouble to understand why it's bad to use weedkillers, why
chemical fertilizers and sprays are poisoning the land and us,' he
continues. 'I want to leave something positive for my children
and theirs.' He grows grass under the vines and works carefully
to help the vines produce lots of leaves for sucessful photo-
synthesis and few bunches, so as to concentrate the plant's energies. 'This is not a nine to five kind of job,' he says, shaking his
head. 'If bad weather threatens, I've been known to spray my
vines with copper sulphate at night or on Sundays to protect
them, because if you're not using chemicals you have to be
much more vigilant or you'll lose your crop.' His yields are low:
in 2008 he produced just 200 quintals of grapes from his ten
hectares of vines.

Damijan doesn't yet have a cellar equipped to accommodate
amphoræ, so he macerates his grapes in low, open-topped conical wooden barrels for 60 to 90 days or more before ageing the
wines for many years in large wooden barrels. 'Making macerated wines from grapes that have not been chemically treated is
a return to a more harmonious, slower-paced experience of life,'
he explains. 'One that was used by our forefathers and theirs,
without causing damage to the environment. All I need to
extract the fruit from my grapes' skins is warmth and time, and
those are easy to find if you're prepared not to compromise.' As
he has discovered, wines made using this approach are not
always immediately understood by drinkers whose expectations
about white wines may still be for colourless – or almost – liquids. 'If you leave ripe, golden grapes to macerate, you get rich-
ly coloured, amber wines.' Initially that philosophy caused problems too with the institutions that grant the DOC status, who
consistently failed the wines on their colour alone, despite the
extraordinary care Damijan (and others in similar situations)
take in the making of their wines. Luckily the disciplinare
changed in 2007, and colour is no longer a factor in the judging
of the wines.

'If you are open to wine as an experience, you'll appreciate
these for their purity and ability to transmit the beauty and minerality of our land and its fruits,' he says. I agree and so do the

*Opposite: Damijan
Podversic*

growing number of drinkers who are fans of this approach. His wines, such as Bianco Kaplja, of Chardonnay, Tocai and Malvasia Istriana, are individual, energized and elegant, with the delicate notes of exoticism that have become his trademark.

Wine
Primosic

Madonnina d'Oslavia, 3
Oslavia
TEL 0481 635153
www.primosic.com

Marko Primosic's motto is 'Think yellow!' He's so into the colour that he even had his sports car custom-sprayed. Why? 'The Ribolla Gialla grape is a bright yellow, a mellow yellow, and it's unique to the Collio, the symbol of a viticulture that gives its best in this terroir,' he says. The Primosic family make two wines from their Ribolla, a fresh immediately drinkable version vinified only in steel, and a lightly macerated (by Oslavia standards) wine left on the skins for around six days before being aged in wooden barrels, called Ribolla di Oslavia. Silvestro Primosic, Marko's father, has a twinkle in his eye as he savours the 'fresh' Ribolla. 'You see how clean, how drinkable this is,' he says, 'it's young, elegant and light, and it goes well with food which is what a wine should do.'

It's harvest time, September 2008, and this is Silvestro's 53rd *vendemmia*. We're out on the terrace, overlooking the hills that were a battle ground in the First World War. 'At that time, everything here was completely destroyed,' says Silvestro, shaking his head. 'For three years this was no-man's land. After 500 years of Austrian rule, the *comune* was removed by force and all its documents destroyed. There's not a single pre-1920 building left standing.' The Primosics have been on this land since the 1700's; Silvestro's grandfather ran his own farm and was self-sufficient; the modern-day family has 26 hectares of Collio vineyards. 'The problem really came later,' he says. 'We in this area

Silvestro Primosic and his son, Marko

Ribolla Gialla

went from being the south of a huge northern empire and, as such, valued for our products, sun and culture, to being the northernmost part of a country in which no one wanted us or what we produced any more, and this crisis lasted until the 1960s.' The Primosic family were among the first to bottle their wines, starting in the late 1950s; when the Collio Consortium was founded, in 1964, Primosic was allocated number 1, its first *bollino*. The family's affiliation with the Consortium continues: Marko is currently one of its vice-presidents as well as commercial director of the family firm. His brother, Boris, helps Silvestro in the vineyards and with the winemaking.

Walking me through their vineyards, the Primosics explain that each parcel of land here has its own name. 'In the old days you walked everywhere, so every terrain was known by its name, like Klin,' says Silvestro. Klin turns out to be an astonishingly steep vineyard that faces north-east and swoops all the way down below Oslavia to the border with Slovenia. Primosic makes a single-vineyard, mixed-grape wine from it called, not surprisingly, Klin, a Collio Bianco DOC blend. This contains Sauvignon, Chardonnay, Ribolla and Tocai Friulano. Tasting both the 2004 and the 1999, I remark on how well the older vintage is showing. 'That's one of the Collio's hidden aces,' says Silvestro proudly. 'Our wines often improve over time thanks to their earthy minerality, it's just hard to make people understand it's sometimes worth putting down their white wines, as they would their reds.'

Wine

Dario Princic

Via Ossario, 15
Oslavia
TEL 0481 532730

When I first visited Dario Princic it was just getting dark, an evening in September that was beginning to show the autumn chill. Down under the back of Dario's farmhouse at Oslavia is a small *frasca*, a tiny bar where the locals – mostly old men on that visit – gather to have a glass of wine and eat a few slices of hand-made *salame* or cheese. Inside are other, larger vaulted rooms for tasting wines or having a meal prepared by Dario's wife Franca.

Dario waits till the grapes are super-ripe before picking, and then macerates them on the skins in open-topped vats for periods that go from six to twenty days for the whites, thirty to forty for the reds. A member of the Vini Veri group, Dario asserts: 'We try to make wines that are as natural as possible. This involves using only manure to fertilize; planting grass under the vines and avoiding all weedkillers; and using only sulphur and copper to spray the vines against disease and pests.' This sounded like standard organic principles, but Dario assured me their group pratice more stringent controls under an auto-certification procedure in which each producer vouches for himself. 'We also go for wild yeasts, and never innoculate using selected yeasts,' he says. The wines are aged in wooden barrels of different sizes and ages. Here are my notes on the Chardonnay 2002, tasted in 2006: Almost yolk-yellow in colour, with saffron highlights. The perfumes jump out at you: notes of orange, rich apricots; earthy and very complex with hints of Mediterranean herbs, wild fennel. Big evolution and fullness in the mouth, a note of tar, noble rot; long finale. Others in the series include Jakot, Pinot Grigio, Ribolla Gialla and Bianco Trbez; Merlot and Cabernet Sauvignon. These are wines for the adventurous taster!

Wine
Radikon

Tre Buchi, 4
Oslavia
TEL 0481 32804
www.radikon.it

The last time I visited Stanislao Radikon – Stanko for short – he was in the midst of what looked like a battleground. It was harvest-time up in Oslavia and his family and workers were picking in a sloping vineyard surrounded by woods. They were not the first to reach the juicy ripe grapes: a herd of wild boar had beaten them to it. Stanko took me around the perimeter of the vineyard, showing me what looked like mud slides the boar had used as access. In some cases vines had been rooted from below as the boar dug for grubs and bulbs. Mostly it was the bunches that had suffered; parts of the rows had been stripped of their fruit.

'Almost everyone else has long since finished harvesting around here, so all the boar descend on my place,' he said, shaking his head. 'It's a serious problem. The boar population is growing exponentially and there's little we can do about it.'

2008 was also a complicated year for growers who oppose chemical warfare against the vine's other enemies, pests and fungus. Peronospera, or mildew, threatened early in the season due to weeks of wet weather. 'I won't spray systemic chemicals on my land,' says Stanko. 'Even if the cost is losing portions of the crop.' Radikon uses copper and sulphur, as well as treatments based on propolis and some types of flour to draw the humidity away from the grapes. His motto is 'natural with no compromises' and he sticks to it. Indeed, Radikon has even taken the courageous step of banning sulphites from the cellar. 'The difference is not only in the purity of the wine, it's also in its openness and expressivity, which really increase when sulphites are not used. I don't condemn their use, but I prefer to do without,' he says while admitting that this decision carries the risk of some bottles remaining unstable over time.

'Making wine is like any other major decision, it implies making life choices,' Stanko says. 'We live in a truly beautiful natural area, but most people just don't see that using chemical weedkillers, fertilizers and so on compromise the health of this land and its future. We take a lot of criticism for what are seen as radical decisions, but I feel too strongly about these issues to mind what others think.' He adds that it's not enough to be certified organic or biodynamic, as those movements allow many treatments for soil and plants that he would never use. 'You need to sensitize people rather than just certify them!'

Stanko Radikon drives the tractor while his son Sasa loads grapes during the harvest

Radikon has also taken a stand on his method of vinification. Like a handful of local producers – including Josko Gravner, La Castellada and Damijan Podversic – Stanko gives his white grapes long macerations on the skins in order to extract more flavour and character. 'There's nothing new about this,' he says. 'I have a Slovenian book from 1844 that talks of making wine the way we do. Many producers criticize us for the style of wines we make, but lots of them are doing experiments in maceration in their cellars. In order to really capture the identity of a terroir in your wines, you need to give them time to evolve. We have white wines aged 10, 15, even 20 years in our cellar that are still alive and vibrant. It's odd that great red wines are judged through time, but not whites.' The Radikons do very long, slow macerations on the skins that include both the alcoholic and malolactic fermentations in large, conical barrels.

For Radikon, the Collio's future lies in its indigenous grape varieties; they are worth investing in. He has invented a name for Tocai (which as of 2008 can no longer be used): Jakot, or Tokaj backwards. Radikon, with the help of his wife, Suzana and son, Sasa, currently makes four wines: Ribolla Gialla; Jakot; Oslavje (a blend of Chardonnay, Pinot Grigio and Sauvignon); and Merlot, all bottled as IGT Venezia Giulia. Radikon made the radical decision to design a special bottle for his wines, in 500ml and 1-litre sizes, with narrow necks for thinner corks, to reduce the risk of oxidisation. The Jakot 2003, tasted in 2008, was a burnished apricot colour, with more apricots to the nose. It opened like a flower, with hints of sweet Marsala and resinous Mediterranean herbs, and evolved, natural and all of a piece, in the palate and long mineral finale: a beautiful, personal wine that would only improve with food.

Wine
Matijaz Tercic

Bucuje, 9
San Floriano del Collio
TEL 0481 884193
www.tercic.com

'Up here, in the *comune* of San Floriano, we get the Bora winds blowing down from Slovenia in spring in autumn,' says Matijaz Tercic as we walk down through a sloping vineyard below his cellar. In spring and summer that can help dry the grapes after a rain, but it makes winter pruning much colder.

A century and a half ago, Tercic's grandparents were *coloni*, or tenant farmers, for two noble landowners. 'They bought a few little pieces of land whenever they could,' explains Matijaz, 'and even though that means we don't now have our vineyards in a single plot, it gives us an assortment of terrains to plant on.' The vines, too, are of mixed ages, with some 40-year-old Merlots among the oldest.

Opposite: Oslavia's war monument dominates the autumn vineyards

Matijaz, who is himself in his early forties, is a third-generation grower, but only began bottling in 1993. 'When I joined my father, we laboured all year to grow good grapes only to sell them at harvest time. That upset me as it made our work seem incomplete. So we started to produce a little wine and within a few years were no longer selling grapes at all.' This gradual step into winemaking has allowed them to expand slowly, which Tercic sees as an advantage.

To have the space to work well, the Tercics have recently completed a large new cellar building, with panoramic views towards Oslavia and beyond. In the foreground is a steep, crescent-shaped vineyard that is planted in double rows to Chardonnay, with Pinot Grigio below it. 'This is one of our more recent vineyards, and our yields here are less than 1 kilo per plant,' explains the soft-spoken Matijaz, whose features are decidedly Slovenian. 'The estate totals 8.2 hectares, of which two are rented from neighbours.' The large tasting room was designed to accommodate groups of up to twenty people. Matijaz's wife, Miriam, sees to the administrative side of the business, and looks after their three daughters, Ana, Klara and Edith. With help from a regional youth-opportunities programme, they have hired a young man to help with the work. Matijas has been a member of the Consortium's council.

The winery's output has now reached 35,000 bottles, most of which are white. Chardonnay, Sauvignon, Pinot Grigio and Ribolla Gialla are bottled separately. There are also white blends: Vino degli Orti is an IGT of mixed Tocai and Malvasia; Collio Bianco is of 90% Chardonnay picked when the grapes are very ripe, and 10% late-harvest Pinot Bianco; this is the only wine that is barrel aged and bottled unfiltered. It drinks well for several years. In good vintages a little Pinot Bianco is produced from a 'too often forgotten' German clone, Geisenham, obtained from the Geisenham winemaking institute.

'Each winemaking family here must decide what style of wine they want to make, and we are no exception,' he says. 'My approach is not to make them heavy or overly extracted but to look for elegance and longevity in wines that reflect the territory.' Since 2003 he destalks the berries before pressing, to remove the tannic, bitter and green influences of the stalks. This allows the grapes' polyphenols and anthocyans to remain intact. Tercic now also macerates all his grapes in the press for short periods at controlled temperatures. Just the amount of grapes needed to fill the press are picked at one time, usually in the cool of the morning. Tercic decides when to pick by tasting the grapes. 'Before we began using these techniques we used to vinify everything '*in bianco*', as in Burgundy,' he says. 'Now we have developed a style that is our own.'

Wine

Valerisce, 6/a
San Floriano del Collio
TEL 0481 884215
www.francoterpin.it

Terpin

Franco Terpin is an organic grower whose winery sits high above the Valerisce valley at San Floriano. On the wall of his current cellar under the house – he's in the process of building a big new one which should be finished in 2009 – there's a grainy old black and white photo of two cows pulling a plough to create a vineyard. 'We're trying to turn the clock back in terms of working the land,' says the young man, who has the appearance of a gentle giant. 'But nowadays an independent producer like myself has to be not only a viticulturalist, but also do PR and run the commercial side of the business. It's increasingly difficult for small winemakers in this ever more globalized world.'

Terpin makes 20,000 bottles and feels that small producers can only stand out from the bigger estates that control the market through the personality of their wines. 'By working the land ourselves we can make wines with the flavours they once had.' Terpin has ten hectares in ten plots that are scattered around the Collio, with three in Slovenia. His approach to the land combines diverse natural techniques. Weedkillers are banned; the vines' leaves are sprayed with energizing infusions of nettle and equisette; composted mulches are given, such as of fermented vine prunings. The French phytobiologist, Michel Barbaud is a consultant to Terpin's work. 'Our aim is to reactivate the soils. Sometimes we've left them for ten years under grass,' he says. 'However, the choices we've made have not always been understood by others. Our macerated wines have sometimes been rejected simply on the grounds of their deep colours.'

These natural methods can make for hard choices. In damp, rainy vintages, the vines are extremely vulnerable to all kinds of disorders, some of which may destroy the grapes; it takes courage and conviction to refrain from using systemic products to save them. 'My father's generation experienced the boom of chemical products that seemed miraculous at the time. Only later did they realize that what poisons the land can be bad for our health too,' he says. 'So in a difficult year, I have to fight with him, but after ten years of banishing those products, I'm not turning back.'

How did the estate develop? 'My father and I made the decision to switch from mixed agriculture – with a few barnyard animals and crops – to vinegrowing in 1980,' he says. 'Then in 1990 we stopped selling our grapes when their prices dropped

Opposite: Valerisce vine-yards in late autumn like a Missoni weave

so dramatically, and opened a small *frasca* here in the cellar, where people could stop in for a glass of wine around the fire-place. At the time it was illegal to serve food with the wine, but everybody did it. It was the only way to survive in what were extremely hard times.'

Franco Terpin is always to be found in the vineyards. He does the lion's share of the work himself, helped by his now eighty-year-old father and young nephew, Erik – to keep the male line of the family going, as Franco and his wife Daniela have two young daughters. He made his first attempts at macerating the wines in 2001, and changed over completely to these methods in 2006. With the assistance of Barbaud and of Marinka Polencic, a Collio œnologist, Terpin aims to emphasize the 'feminine' side of his wines. 'In very long macerations this fragrance can some-times be lost, so I prefer to do a four-day maceration on the skins, as in this 2005 Jakot – a Tocai,' he says.

His other wines include Stamas Bianco, a white Collio blend named for its vineyard. Here Terpin does a pre-harvest selection of the ripest grapes and macerates them for four to five days to start the fermentation. When the rest of the grapes are harvest-ed, they are added to these starter yeasts. 'We allow them to decant naturally for a night, and then ferment this clean must in large barrels. After one year in barrel, the wine is moved to steel vats for another year, then fined in the bottle for a final year.' The unfiltered wine comes out reactive and long, with good minerality.

Single-varietal wines are made from whole or very lightly crushed berries. They are fermented in open-topped conical barrels, with the cap pushed down four to five times daily, but not left long enough to take on too much tannin. The wines follow the same three-year cycle as the Stamas. Siralis is the top line, followed by Stamas and Quinto Quarto, which come out as Vini da Tavola.

The new underground cellar is surrounded by woods, and will give the Terpins much more space. Upstairs the tasting room commands great views of the landscape: future plans include a few rooms for agriturismo guests.

Giasbana

Agriturismo

Kovac

Giasbana, 11
San Floriano del Collio
TEL 0481 390247
www.kovackorsic.com

Zvonka and Rudi Korsic have turned their small farm into a welcoming and very affordable agriturismo. Each of the four apartments has its own kitchen, and includes outdoor tables under the shady trees for summer dining. Zvonka is a lovely hostess and prepares delicious breakfasts for those who prefer not to cook their own. This is a perfect place for children who love animals, as the farm has cats, dogs, and donkeys. Open all year. The Korsics produce some wine too and their son, Fabjan, is an active member of the Consortium's council.

Restaurant

Luka Trattoria

Giasbana, 16
San Floriano del Collio
TEL 0481 391704
CLOSED Monday,
Tuesday
PRICE €€€

Luka is modernist, stylish and fun. Its design is completely different from the wooden-beamed interiors of its local cousins. Where else would you find a luminous dining room overlooking the vineyards painted Magritte-apple green? Or such eclectic detailing in the décor? It's so pretty it would fit into any cosmopolitan city. Luka was once a traditional, middle of the road eatery, but since Patrizia Felluga took it over in early 2008 it's become a much more attractive spot to stop in for lunch, dinner or a drink. In warm weather eat out under the garden pergola or join the local winemakers for a glass of Collio Bianco at the stand-up bar on the terrace. The idea here is to showcase the blended whites that carry the Collio's name, and that vary so much in their approaches. As for the food, it's evolving into a seasonal menu that includes salads and cold platters of cheeses and cured meats, and hot dishes taken from traditional recipes. It's located almost directly across the road from the little white church at Giasbana, above the vineyards of Zuani.

Giasbana wineries

Wine

Gradis'ciutta

Giasbana, 10
San Floriano del Collio
TEL 0481 390237
www.gradisciutta.com

Robert Princic's large new cantina is located just down the hill from the white church at Giasbana. 'We are right near what was the wartime border between Yugoslavia and Italy and, in 1947, a cantina was offered to this community to use as a church after the war. Later, a new church was erected here, so for us it holds special significance,' Robert explains. Until 1997 Robert's father, Isidoro Princic, made wine to sell wholesale to other bottlers from a large warehouse on the site of what is now the family's cellar. There are five Princic families bottling wine in the Collio.

'I had finished studying œnology,' says Robert, 'and wanted to come back and join the family. My father was delighted as he didn't want to undertake making and bottling our own wines by himself.' The Princics invested in the vineyards and in converting the old building. In 1997 they selected the name Gradis'ciutta in

*Opposite: Isidoro Princic
and his son Robert*

*A colourful old cement
wine vat at Gradis'ciutta*

honour of the tiny village nearby, confusingly spelt Gradiscutta.

Robert and his fiancé, Katja, work alongside the Princic parents running the wine business, with vineyards in several locations of the Collio, from Ruttars in the north to Monte Calvario, south of the winery. Robert is also a councillor for the Consortium. They started with nine hectares of vines in 1997, but now own thirty hectares of land, of which eighteen are vineyards, with an annual production of 100,000 bottles.

'I find that Pinot Grigio and Chardonnay prefer cooler situations,' explains Robert as we take a drive to Monte Calvario to visit his vineyards there, where he's planted these varieties behind a row of olive trees. Up on the slopes of Monte Calvario above Lucinico it is Ribolla Gialla and Malvasia that flourish. 'This large vineyard was abandoned when we took it over, and we've gradually been putting it in order; it has a special microclimate.' The Princics are also proud of the vineyards they have recently bought and redone between Ruttars and Plessiva, shaped like a steep amphitheatre.

Robert is considering converting some of his vineyards to organic methods, but says he'll have to start slowly and see how it goes. He's looking for balance in both his methods and his wines. His two white Collio blends, Tùzz and Bràtinis, are among his most successful wines. Tùzz, a Riserva mix of Malvasia, Chardonnay and Tocai Friulano is fermented first in steel and then in the large wooden barrels used for its ageing, as its golden yellow colour attests. Bràtinis is a blend of very ripe Chardonnay, Sauvignon and Ribolla Gialla worked exclusively in steel and then aged on the lees. Originally a wine reserved for the family's special occasions, it is now made in small quantities for their customers to enjoy.

Wine and Olive Oil
Alessio Komjanc

Giasbana, 35
San Floriano del Collio
TEL 0481 391228
www.mtvfriulivg.com

The family-run Komjanc winery is on the windy road that rises from Preval towards Giasbana, in a strip of land that borders with Slovenia. 'Most of the property owners here are of Slovenian origin,' explains Roberto Komjanc, 'whereas in Preval and going towards Isonzo they're more Italian.' The family is originally from San Floriano, and are now in their fifth generation of *contadini* working the land. Roberto's father, Alessio, moved from San Floriano with his sons in 1976 to set up a farm of his own. 'I was nine years old at the time,' says Roberto. 'We had started bottling by then and I loved accompanying my father to the trattorias of Trieste and Grado to sell our wines,' he says.

The estate has grown from 18 to 27 hectares, of which 22 are

Raffaella Komjanc and her son in her flower garden

Roberto Komjanc and his son

registered to Collio DOC. Since joining his father and brothers Benjamino, Ivan and Patrik in 2000, Roberto and his wife Raffaella have handled the commercial side of the business. 'My father is always happier in the vineyards, as is my brother Ivan.' They are helped in the cellar by the consultant, Alvano Moreale, from Casarsa. Production has risen fast: from 15,000 bottles in 2000 to 128,000 in 2008. 'We've always had a good market locally for our wines, which are reasonably priced, but now we want to expand by doing some trade fairs too,' says Roberto. They are currently producing two lines of wines: Classic, with pale labels and eleven single-variety wines, and the higher blue-label collection of seven wines, including a Spumante and a Picolit. All the whites are worked exclusively in stainless steel. Roberto, his wife, and their small son, Mosé, are very hospitable and keen to receive guests at the winery, for tastings and cellar visits.

'I'm very interested in the diversity of the indigenous grape varieties we have here,' says Roberto. 'There are far more than the three – Ribolla Gialla, Malvasia and Tocai – that we hear most about.' He studied viticulture at Udine and, in collaboration with the university, has planted an experimental vineyard with one row each of eighteen rare cultivars, including Cividìn, Cordenons, Negrat, Mariabin, and Givan. 'There's not enough of each to really vinify them separately, but we wanted to help keep them going.'

The Komjancs also sell extra virgin olive oil from their own olive trees at San Floriano. The olive varieties they work with, some of which are special to the area, are: Maurino, Leccino, Casaliva, Frantoio, Pendolino e Bianchera.

Wine
Skok

Giasbana, 15
San Floriano del Collio
TEL 0481 390280
www.skok.it

The Skok siblings are a sympathetic pair. 'When I was a child I wanted to be a *contadina*, and I was the first one to learn how to drive the tractor,' says the lively Orietta, who was born in 1967, three years before her brother Edi.

'That's true,' he replies, 'but I prefer working in the cellar anyway.'

'That's fine with me,' she laughs, because all there is to do in the cellar is wash, wash, wash!'

They started young, earning 100 lire per row after school for pruning and other jobs in the vineyard, helping their father and uncle, Giuseppe and Armando, on the farm. There were cherries to sell in May along the roadside (for 1,000 lire per kilo) gathered from the orchard's then hundred cherry trees. Now only seventeen remain but they still sell the fruit in good years.

Orietta Skok at their villa

Their father died when Edi was almost eighteen, and for the

next decade Orietta and Edi ran the estate with their uncle until he, too, died. Now the two of them manage the winery alone. Their mother, Erminia, tends to the lovely flower and vegetable gardens. A new generation has already begun: Edi's son, Nikolaj, was born in 2007.

'Our family can be traced back on this land for 500 years,' says Orietta, 'but they were *mezzadri* – tenant farmers – until 1968, when our parents and uncle bought the estate, of which only three hectares were vineyards.'

The property surrounds the large Villa Jasbinae, the former-summer house of the Count Teuffenbach who owned large portions of the surrounding hills. 'The Attems family also lived here in the 1750s,' explains Edi. 'Unfortunately we don't know much more than that as the archives at San Floriano were lost in a fire.'

Life was hard in the 1970s as the family sold their grapes to pay back the mortgage, a market that was very poorly paid. There was little to eat outside of what could be home-grown. Later it was must that was sold. 'I really wanted us to start making our own wine,' says Edi, 'and in 1991 we began bottling.'

The Skok estate now totals eighteen hectares, of which eleven are vineyards and seven fields and woods. 80 percent of the wines are divided between four whites: Pinot Grigio, Sauvignon, Chardonnay and Tocai; Merlot makes up the rest in two versions, with and without the use of wooden barrels. Edi says he likes to keep his work on the wines to a minimum, cooling the must to 12° or 13°C before a natural decantation, then adding selected yeasts; the white varietals are made exclusively in stainless steel. Bianco Pe.Ar is dedicated to the two Skok brothers who began the farm, Pepi and Armando. Tocai Zabura or Zeta, a blend, is named for the Tocai Friulano cru.

Wine

Zuani

Giasbana, 12
San Floriano del Collio
TEL 0481 391432
www.zuanivini.com

Patrizia Felluga's estate, Zuani, is located a stone's throw from the white church at Giasbana. Patrizia is one of Friuli's foremost women wine producers, and has been making award-winning wines since she set up her own business in 2001. Until then she had helped her father, Marco Felluga, run the family's other wineries (see p. 117 and p. 223). She was looking for a new challenge.

'I grew up in a family entirely committed to winemaking and I'd always lived that life,' she says. 'But after a long time working with my parents, I realized I wanted to do something new that would tie me more directly to the *territorio*.' Patrizia

*Patrizia Felluga in front
of her cellar*

consulted with her son, Antonio, who now helps run Zuani, her
daughter, Caterina, and of course with her father. 'I remember
he said: "Don't think that buying a wine estate is as easy as
buying a pair of shoes!" But I was determined and had a clear
idea of what I wanted to do,' she says. 'My father's amazing!
His heart may have skipped a beat when I told him I wanted to
change, but he quickly got behind the idea and helped me in
every way he could, pushing me to be more ambitious. That's
one of his great qualities,' she says, smiling.

Both Marco and Patrizia Felluga have long been champions of
the Collio Bianco project: the white Collio blend whose first disciplinare was approved in 1968. 'I realized there was little point
in my producing another Pinot Grigio just to make money,' she
says. 'I feel that the Collio blend can offer us a unique, place-
specific wine that really stands out from the varietal-driven
whites that Italy is full of.'

When she found it, Zuani was a 4.5-hectare farm on the eastern border of the Collio that overlooked the Slovenian hills. The
property is situated on a softly rounded hilltop, with the vineyards sloping away below it in all directions, and is well
exposed and ventilated. The *contadino* who lived there had
planted the vines to four varieties, Friulano, Sauvignon,
Chardonnay and Pinot Grigio, and she decided to keep them.
'My first harvest was from these grapes, though there was no
real cellar, just a large building that had been used to store farm
equipment. I cleared it out, brought in four steel tanks and four
barriques, and we were off!'

The following year she had time to analyze the soil in different parts of the estate, and to plan for future plantings with the
help of the Piemontese consultant, Donato Lanati, who had col-
laborated with the Felluga family. The estate now has grown to

ten hectares. As for the blend, its proportions follow the wine's project design, varying slightly with each harvest. 'There's nothing pre-planned,' she says. 'Sometimes I can tell from the outset which varieties are going well together, but mostly I vinify each variety separately and blend later.' What is interesting about Patrizia's decision is that she makes just one wine in two versions: Zuani Vigne is vinified exclusively in stainless steel, and comes out in the May following the harvest. It's a clean, fruit-driven wine that is proving to be a big prizewinner. Zuani (Patrizia often calls this wine Zuani Zuani) has the same starting point but here the must is fermented and aged in wooden barrels for nine months, followed by one year in the bottle; it is sold in the summer. Zuani Zuani is bottled unfiltered, and is a much more complex wine, meant for longer ageing, with depth and a wonderfully zingy finale.

Patrizia Felluga is active on many fronts in the Collio. She is currently the president of the Collio Consortium, and has recently also taken over the trattoria, Luka (see p. 90) that overlooks her estate at Giasbana, infusing it with the sophisticated sense of style she says she has inherited from her mother.

Patrizia Felluga with her son Antonio

'I really believe in this area,' she says as we look out over her neat vineyards from her cellar's high viewpoint. 'Being so close to the east may once have been a handicap as we were quite cut off from modernisation, but now I see it as a blessing as it has protected the authenticity that can be found in the Collio's wines and their makers.'

OTHER WINERIES
Castel San Mauro – Manuele Mauri
Castel San Mauro, 1, San Mauro; tel 0481 534164
Francesco and Claudio Komic
Gradiscutta, 15; tel 0481 390763
Emilio Sfiligoj
Via Lenzuolo Bianco, 6, San Floriano del Collio; tel 0481 32521
Emilio Terpin
Scedina, 22, San Floriano Del Collio; tel 0481 884044
Nikolaj Simon Komjanc
Uclanzi 4/A, San Floriano del Collio; tel 0481 884096
Ivan Vogric
Uclanzi, 16, San Floriano Del Collio; tel 0481 884152;
Humar–Marcello and Marino Humar
Valerisce, 2, San Floriano del Collio; tel 0481 884094
Marega–Livio and Giorgio Marega
Valerisce, 4 , San Floriano del Collio; tel 0481 884058

Chapter 2

Mossa, San Lorenzo Isontino and Capriva del Friuli

From Lucinico, via Mossa, San Lorenzo Isontino, Capriva del Friuli and Spessa to Russiz

In this chapter we move through the *comuni* of Mossa, San Lorenzo Isontino and Capriva del Friuli to visit the gentle hills of Spessa and Russiz. This is an area fully dedicated to vineyards, interspersed with patches of woods. Its notable landmarks include the Castello di Spessa and Villa Russiz, both important wineries featured in this chapter. Close by Villa Russiz, surrounded by vines and trees, is the cupola-topped mausoleum of Théodore de La Tour, whose French influence proved so important to the area's winemaking.

Lucinico

Honey

Via Cicuta, 1
Lucinico
TEL 0481 535624
lacasadellape@tin.it

Opposite: Marco Perco of Roncùs removing unwanted shoots in spring

La Casa dell'Ape

This is the headquarters for a cooperative of 19 beekeepers and honey-gatherers whose hives are set up in the Collio and Carso hills. The members gather their honey as the flowering plants come into season – from delicate Collio acacia and lime *(tiglio)* to Carso wild cherry *(marasca)* and deep-flavoured chestnut *(castagna)*. They also produce propolis, pollen and other bee-related foods and supplements. While the cooperative does not sell directly to the public here, its products can be found in local

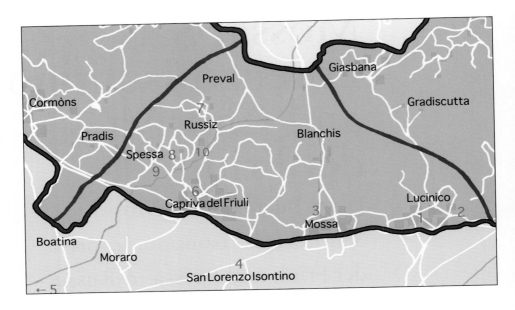

markets, grocery shops and in some wineries, including Angoris (see pp. 135-136).

Pastry shop and bakery
Pasticceria Azzano

Piazza San Giorgio, 40
Lucinico
TEL 0481 390171

This is my favourite pasticceria in the area. It's bang in the centre of the town, on the main road to Gorizia. It dates back to 1931 and has always been run by the same family, who milled the wheat, baked the bread and made the delicious desserts. Inside the broad-fronted shop is a sumptuous display of strudels, cakes and pastries in the gleaming showcases. Stop in for a coffee or cake at a table, or do as the locals do: buy *un vassoio* (a trayful) of pastries to take away. Don't miss their coiled Gubana di Gorizia, a 18th-century pastry stuffed with nuts and dried fruits, or any of the mittel-European cakes, including marbled Cugluf, spiral Putizza, or fried Crafen doughnuts. Azzano is open all day, so stop in for breakfast, a sandwich at lunch, a cake with tea, or an evening aperitivo.

Restaurant, Wine
Giorgio Grion

Via Sartorio, 75
Lucinico
TEL 0481 390355
giorgio.grion@libero.it
OPEN Fri, Sat, Sun from
October to May
PRICE €€

Giorgio Grion and his family run a lively, rustic osteria – or *ristoro agrituristico* – named Grion, near one of the train underpasses in Lucinico. They produce their own wine for it, from 3.5 hectares of vineyards, half of which are in the Collio DOC. I discovered that Giorgio is a man of many interests: not only is he a keen photographer, but he is also a specialist on medieval music and dances; his folk-dancing group, Danzerini di Lucinico, often performs at Gorizia's annual folk fair in late August. This exploration of ancient local customs spreads to food. The Grion's restaurant sometimes organizes dinners using Friuli recipes from centuries past.

'Our research into classic dishes from this part of the country is partly thanks to my grandmother, Elisabetta,' he says as we sample some of the Grions' home-cured prosciutto and a glass of delicious Picolit, made in the *amabile* style. 'She was a *contadina*, but she had a friend who cooked for the local bishop and taught her many special dishes.' Giorgio also collects old cookbooks, some of them manuscript collections.

Giorgio Grion at the agriturismo

The restaurant, with its simple wooden tables and friendly atmosphere, is located in a house built in 1992 next to the family's older residence. It's a good place to sample some of the local specialities that illustrate the area's mittel-European influences, from noodles with Speck ham and poppy seeds, to pork sausages with the pickled turnips known as *brovada*. Desserts include home-made pear and chocolate strudel and la Gubana, the dried fruit-filled ring cake. Giorgio's sister, Maria Luisa, and nieces, Elisabetta and Eleonora, and nephew, Massimiliano, help run the osteria, while his father, Sergio, still drives the tractor and handles much of the vineyard work. Sergio is a wonderful, lively character, full of colourful stories about the agricultural past of the area. 'You need to be at least thirty years old to make wine,' he says. 'Young peoples' palates are not experienced enough. In my youth it was the old men who poured out the doses of grappa to keep us warm in the woods and fields when the icy Bora wind was blowing.' Sergio is an expert *grappista*, and explained how it was made under cover after the war. The first and hottest part, or 'head' of the grappa was discarded from the 'heart', or drinking grappa; it was infused with salt and spices and used as rubbing alcohol to cure aches and pains.

Sergio worked with his father as a nurseryman and is an expert at grafting vines. He treasures the lessons learned in his youth. 'In those days, when we ordered from a nursery, we specified the type of rootstock we wanted, not the variety of grape, and did our own grafting. That was before the advent of weedkillers, which have done so much to kill the areas's fauna too. Here the countryside was full of hare and pheasants, toads,

*Lucinico seen from
Monte Calvario*

lizards and snakes, all of which were healthy for the vineyards,' he says, wistfully. The Grions are keen on maintaining some of the native grapes from the area, and make wines from white Cividìn, and from the reds Pignolo and Tazzelenghe.

Wine

Via Giulio Cesare, 36/a
Lucinico
TEL 0481 393619
www.attems.it

Attems

If the Collio can be said to owe its identity as a specific wine-making area to any individual, that person is undoubtedly the late Count Douglas Attems. His ideas about the Collio territory, its grape varieties and their potential were decades ahead of their time, and the repercussions of those ideas are still being felt today. The historic Attems estate dates from 1100, and is the Collio's oldest. Records show that wine was made on the large farm in the 16th century, and probably much earlier. Sadly, the family's imposing country house at Piedimonte was destroyed in the First World War; Douglas Attems' daughter, Virginia, still lives in what was once the property's lodge, itself a handsome villa at Lucinico.

It was after Second World War that Attems began to modern-ize his vineyards and conceive a plan for uniting the area's viti-cultural forces. At that time each small tenant holding had some vineyards in amongst other crops. Attems saw the great results the vines on the hillsides of the Collio gave and formulated a way to delineate those hills as a separate entity from the flat plains whose soils were different and less suited to growing grapes. He united then under the banner of the Collio denomi-nation and, in 1964, founded the Consortium.

'My father made the transition here from a mixed farm to one specialized in winemaking, and he often put the Collio's inter-ests ahead of his own,' says Virginia Attems. 'He always said that on the wines' labels you needed to write the word Collio in large letters and the name of the producer in smaller letters, to emphasize its origins.' As president of the Collio Consortium, a position he held for 35 years, Attems became an active ambassa-dor for the Collio and its wines. His ideas for the Consortium were inspired, and included setting up a technical advisory group to support the small producers in their efforts to improve their vineyards and winemaking skills. 'He understood that only if everyone improved together could the territory's standards be raised,' she says.

Towards the end of his life Attems looked for a partner to help expand and improve his own large estate. After a couple of unsuccessful tries he found a suitable partnership with the Marchesi de' Frescobaldi, one of Tuscany's key wine-producing

families. 'When I first came to visit the estate with my father
and uncle, we were quite nervous,' says Lamberto Frescobaldi.
'After all, this was the first time we had considered venturing
beyond Tuscany to produce wine. We have always had such passionate feelings about our own lands, and wanted to feel equally
engaged elsewhere.' The Frescobaldis soon became enthusiastic
about the Collio and its wines. As producers primarily known
for their great red wines, the Tuscan family was interested in
expanding its portfolio to whites of an equal status. There was
a lot of work to do, investing in new cellar and farm equipment
as well as gradually renewing some of the estate's 50 hectares
of vineyards. It's an ongoing process. They are helped in it by
the young winemaker, Gianni Napolitano, who trained with
them in Tuscany and in New Zealand. 'We discovered what
the locals already knew: that the Collio's wines are justly
famous within Italy, but less known abroad.' They now
export over 40% of the Attems wines and have raised production to 450,000 bottles.

In addition to a line of single-varietal whites, the estate now
produces a wine that was conceived by Douglas Attems but
never produced in his lifetime: Cicinìs. This is a Collio Bianco
blend of Sauvignon, Friulano and Pinot Bianco. 'In this too
Attems was a pioneer: he felt it was a shame to produce only
varietal wines as they are bought more for the grape than for
the territory,' says Frescobaldi. 'He always wanted the Collio to
take the leading role. And in this age of mass-produced
Sauvignons and Chardonnays from the world over, he was
right.' Another new wine, Cupra Ramato, is a Pinot Grigio
macerated on the skins for 36 hours. The result is a wine of a
burnished, rosy colour. '*Ramato* was the name for Pinot Grigio
under the republic of Venezia,' says Virginia Attems. 'Well into
the 19th century Venetians would ask for '*un'ombra di ramato*'
(a glass of copper-coloured wine) as there was then no technology available to make it white.'

Mossa

Agriturismo, Wine
Villa Codelli

Via Codelli, 15
Mossa
TEL 0481 809285
www.codellifahnenfeld.it

This handsome late 16th-century villa and its surrounding rural
farm buildings, wine cellars and little church have been turned
into a lovely place to spend a few days while visiting the Collio.
The noble Codelli family are also very well set up for weddings,
and can accommodate up to 100 guests for dinners and concert
series. Some of the rooms in the Castaldia building are self-

catering and offer the use of a swimming pool. The Codellis sell their wines on the property.

Honey
Christian Suligoi

Via XXIV Maggio, 14
Mossa
tel 328 0967652
www.ilfavo.com

This talented young beekeeper collects honey from the unspoiled, unpolluted countryside: his chestnut *(castagno)*, lime *(tiglio)* and mixed flower *(mille fiori)* honeys are certified organic.

Restaurant
Trattoria Blanch

Via D. Blanchis, 35
Mossa
TEL 0481 80020
CLOSED Tues eve; Weds
PRICE €€

Blanch is a Collio institution: this trattoria been run by the same family since it opened in 1904. Indeed, in 2004 the Blanch family published a book of its history and role over the last century, illustrated with period photos. It's full of stories of partisan resistance to the Germans, and of the special relationship Blanch's had with the nearby brick factory, and which is soon to be restored by Marco Scolaris (see opposite). The large house on the road to Mossa from Preval is surrounded by woods and vineyards; the capacious dining rooms occupy two sides of the ground floor. In summer there are some outdoor tables under large umbrellas. The menu here is classic, and has barely changed over the decades. Hand-made pasta cut into irregular squares is served with mushrooms, or a runny chicken sauce that is one of the Blanch's signature dishes. *Baccalà* and roasts come accompanied by polenta. *Stinco*, or shank, is popular too. Roast meats tend to be given long cooking times and are representative of the simple preparation that one often finds in the Italian coutryside, where technique is kept to a minimum. Desserts are abundant, and wines local.

Restaurant
Trattoria alle Vecchie Province

Via Zorutti, 16
Mossa
TEL 0481 808693
PRICE €€

This is an old-fashioned osteria known as 'Mic', though the owner's name is Francesco Dilena. It's the kind of village hangout where the locals come to play cards and keep each other's company over a glass of local wine in the warm rooms in winter or under the vine-covered pergola in summer. The menu is full of the hearty, uncomplicated fare of the country: *orzotto* with *baccalà* and Montasio cheese, ravioli filled with potato and herbs with meat sauce, carrot gnocchi with wild boar, as well as traditional salt-cured meats.

San Lorenzo Isontino

Winery

Via Boschetto, 4
San Lorenzo Isontino
TEL 0481 809920
www.scolaris.it

Scolaris Vini

The Scolaris estate has its headquarters and cellars at San Lorenzo, in a handsome 19th-century palazzo. 'Our farming business was begun in 1924 by my grandfather, Giovanni, after he returned from the war in Russia,' explains Marco Scolaris. 'He had Austrian origins but if we look further back, there are also Greek roots to my family. In the 1750s Greek soldiers were brought north by the Turks in an attempt to besiege Vienna, and many fled to the Collio. Indeed, Cormòns' coat of arms has a crescent moon as one of its symbols.'

Scolaris continues: 'Under the Austro-Hungarian empire this area was extremely important for its viticulture. Over 500,000 quintals of grapes were being produced annually in the Collio hills prior to the vines' decimation first by phylloxera in the early 1900s, and then by the bombings in the First World War.'

Marco Scolaris measures the distance between plants for a new vineyard

Only after the war were the Italians able to rebuild their wine markets. At that time, the Scolaris were the first of the big companies to see the potential of the Collio's white wines, and to construct a big market for them. 'My grandfather was well liked by the *contadini* he bought grapes from, who were a mixture of sharecroppers and small freeholders. After the wine was made, it was transported in large barrels, first on horse-drawn carriages and then in company trucks.' It was either sold *sfuso*, or pumped into smaller barrels at the customers' osterie. 'My grandfather was quite a character and a great businessman: he managed to sell wine to all the armies that came through here, including the British and Americans.'

By the late 1940s, Giovanni's son, Giovanni Jr., who had studied œnology at Conegliano, had joined the company and they started attending wine trade fairs. 'My father set up one of the area's earliest in-house bottling plants in 1951,' he says. 'We were then producing about 35,000 hectolitres for the northern Italian market.'

The Scolaris' kept abreast of technological innovations and were among the first in Friuli – with Schiopetto, Attems and Villanova – to use German Seitz screw-presses, which made for much cleaner whites.

'Tastes have changed, but up until the 1980s our customers wanted wines with from 13-15° natural alcohol that were strong and flavourful,' says Scolaris, 'and that was quite different from the Veneto, with its taste for light *vinelli*.'

When Marco, who had studied economics and œnology was 25, his father died. 'I had been primed for this job from childhood,' he says. 'As a boy my father would take me to visit trattorias that were our customers, an important school of life that has stood me in good stead.' He bought out his sisters, and took over.

Modernization has continued to be a positive force in the company, which now produces 600,000 bottles as well as some bulk wine. Of these, 300,000 bottles are made in the Collio, which makes Scolaris one of the Collio's largest vinifiers and bottlers. He still buys grapes from about 70 of the families that sold them to his grandfather, and has 20 hectares of his own vineyards in the Collio. Different lines of wines are now produced at the cellars under separate labels: Borgo Boschetto for the Isonzo IGT wines, and Marco Scolaris for those from the Collio DOC.

Scolaris is particularly proud of his Ocelot. 'This comes from a rare red grape variety that we have rediscovered, a type of Tintoria, which is in the Refosco family and had practically disappeared. My grandfather's generation nicknamed it 'ocelot', or 'little bird' in dialect, as the birds love to eat it when it's ripe at harvest time. It was used to produce a wine that was so hard, tannic and sour that it was practically undrinkable for many years, but we have found a way to tame it by picking it when it is really ripe and ageing it in barriques for six years to soften it. It goes very well with game.' Scolaris also produces an unusual Spumante Brut from Ribolla Gialla grapes.

Marco Scolaris' current project is to renovate a beautiful disused brick factory from 1850 at Mossa, which is surrounded by a large park and river bed that was used for extracting and crushing the clay – a handsome piece of industrial architecture. He plans to turn it into the estate's cultural headquarters. It is already inhabited by a menagerie of unusual animals, including a family of Indochinese pigs. A great place to visit with children.

Restaurant

Trattoria al Piave

Via Cormòns, 6
Corona, Mariano del Friuli
TEL 0481 69003
CLOSED Tues
PRICE €€

This restaurant is a few kilometres outside of San Lorenzo Isontino, going south-west towards Mariano, in the tiny village of Corona. It's on the main but modest road that crosses through this village. You can't miss Trattoria al Piave: a black iron 'trattoria' sign hangs outside. Inside, stop in the red-lacquer bar room for a glass of wine and some prosciutto that is always displayed on its counter; it has an authentic feel of a country village bar. The dining rooms are intimate and cosy, especially in winter when a cheery fire is always burning in the fireplace. The stone walls, wooden beams and lace curtains add to the welcoming atmosphere. The Fermanelli family own and run it. Patrizio is the chef. He specializes in traditional dishes, sometimes given a modernizing twist. To start, there are hearty soups and pastas. I loved the *crespelle* – a sort of pancake – filled with nutmeg-scented pumpkin and topped with browned bechamel. Main courses include slow-roasted veal shanks whose tender meat is served sliced with roast potatoes. The wine list features a selection of the Collio's best.

Chunks of prosciutto make a fine aperitivo snack

Capriva del Friuli, Spessa and Russiz

At Capriva, the houses in the Middle Ages were built in circles around the church, in a walled construction known as *la centa*: they created a defendable structure even in the plain, with the church bell tower doubling as a high vantage point. Parts of this original plan can still be seen today. From Capriva del Friuli, the road leads through vineyards towards Spessa and its castle, and to Russiz.

Restaurant, Wine Shop, Hotel,
Vinnaeria La Baita

Via degli Alpini, 2
Capriva del Friuli
TEL 0481 881024
closed Weds
PRICE €€€

This multi-functional location offers lots of options: stop in for a glass of wine and a slice of prosciutto at the large bar that spills outdoors in summer. Buy a bottle of wine from the shop that has over 800 on its lists, many of which are from the Collio, as one would expect. Eat dinner in the restaurant, with its peaceful outdoor summer terrace, or stay in one of the twelve hotel rooms offering Bed & Breakfast in country modern style. The Vinnaeria belongs to Silvio Jermann (see p. 224), who well understands the needs of the wine tourist.

OTHER AGRITURISMI IN CAPRIVA DEL FRIULI

Ivaldo Orzan (Via Mazzini, 48, Capriva del Friuli; tel 0481 809419) This family run agriturismo prepares home-made *salumi* and rustic dishes of local game and home-reared pork, served with its home-made wines in a dining room that has recently been renovated. Open weekends only.

Da Roc Agriturismo (Via Moraro, 5, Capriva del Friuli; tel 0481 80201. www.vinicoceani.com) This small farm belongs to Renzo Coceani and produces organic wines and serves them with grilled meats, salads and other simple country food. Open for lunch and dinner all year.

Wine
Pighin

Viale Grado, 1
Risano, Pavia di Udine
TEL 0432 675444
www.pighin.com

The Pighin family have two wineries, one in the Grave del Friuli, at Risano, and one in the Collio, at Spessa di Capriva. Theirs is a very large estate, with over 150 hectares in the Grave, and 30 in the Collio. The estate produces over a million bottles in the Grave, and 130,000 in the Collio. There are two separate cellars: at Risano it's vast and impressively techno-logical. 'In order to get the soul from the grapes, you need good equipment,' says Roberto Pighin, who now runs the business with his father Fernando and sister, Raffaella. The loquacious Roberto Pighin is a natural promoter of the Collio's virtues and is active on the Consortium's council.

The family have been improving and enlarging the estate since buying it in 1963. 'My grandfather always maintained that land was always a good investment, even in times when no one seemed to want it,' he says. 'For us, Pinot Grigio is the key grape variety and we have demand for it from all over the world.'

Previous pages: The amphitheatre vineyards of Capriva del Friuli

'In the Collio our vineyards form a natural amphitheatre, facing south towards the sea, yet they are well ventilated by the Bora winds.' The vines are planted 4,200 to the hectare, and trained to Guyot. The in-house winemaker, Paolo Valdesolo, stresses that speed is of the essence when you are bringing in the freshly picked grapes in order to maintain their aromas. They cool the berries to 7° or 8°C before pressing, and then chill the must further, to 4°C before letting it decant. The must is then innoculated with yeasts selected specially for each grape variety. The Pighins only work grapes grown in their own vineyards, vinifying each vineyard separately before blending them into one larger batch before bottling. If the Pighin's range of wines from the Grave is extensive, in the Collio DOC it is restricted to three white monovarietal wines – Sauvignon, Chardonnay and Pinot Grigio – two reds (Merlot and Cabernet), and the pride of the family, a Picolit. This dessert wine has a lovely nose of white flowers and roses, with salt-caramel notes, and is balanced and long in the finish.

Near the estate at Risano is the handsome 17th-century villa that is used to entertain the Pighin's guests (there are plans to create an agriturismo in the future). Next to it is the old cellar for the ageing of the reds. It's real historic treasure, with its well-preserved early farm machines and attic rooms where silkworms were once kept. So is the walled vineyard that was planted in the 1980s with 27 varieties of autochthonous grapes.

Wine, Agriturismo

Roncùs

Via Mazzini, 18
Capriva del Friuli
TEL 0481 809349
www.roncùs.it

Marco Perco's winery is on the eastern edge of Capriva, in an attractive cluster of buildings that includes the family's house and cellars on one side of a central courtyard, and the agriturismo and offices on the other. There's a pretty flower garden and, in the courtyard wall, a narrow gate that leads into a small vineyard located within the town of Capriva. 'This is our only vineyard to be planted on flat ground,' he explains. 'All the rest are in the hills.' Marco's commitment to his collection of sloping vineyards is well known, as are the wines that ensue from them. He's also an active councillor for the Consortium, and a keen promoter of wine tourism in the area.

'I believe that if you work in agriculture, you should take an ethical stance with regards to the earth,' he says. 'Too many people live winemaking indirectly, as a business for moneymaking like any other, without regard for the health of the land and its inhabitants.' Marco's sensitivity to these issues has led him to

Wild flowers and grass in Marco Perco's spring vineyards

set up a code of practice for himself and those working for him: in the vineyards, no chemical fertilizers nor weedkillers are used. Mixed grasses grown beneath the vines are cut twice yearly by hand. Snakes and other wildlife are allowed to live freely. 'I've tried to exclude anything I see as a violence towards my vines and their wines,' he continues. 'And that includes barriques, over-long macerations and selected yeasts, all of which tend to standardize the wines.'

I am particularly interested in Marco's winemaking using the fruit of old vines, aged 40 or more years, from which he produces an award-winning wine called, appropriately, Vecchie Vigne. (It's worth remembering that the Collio's hills were devastated during both World Wars, and therefore vineyards aged over 50 years are very unusual here). 'Working with old vines is both a challenge and a joy,' he says. 'You have to start with the idea that each plant has its own character: it's absurd to think they're all the same. Their roots reach deeply into the soil, so the fruit is mineral-rich and doesn't need to be concentrated. They also do much better in difficult years; treatments can be reduced to a minimum as the vines have found their equilibrium in the soil and thus are less susceptible to illness.' Marco Perco's Vecchie Vigne is a blend of Tocai Friulano, Malvasia and Ribolla Gialla, though the old vineyards often have a few other varieties scattered amongst them. The wine remains three years on the lees in medium to large barrels before being passed through a filter wide enough to allow micro-organisms to remain.

'It was when I tasted some French *vieilles vignes* wines that I began to think of doing a wine like that,' he says. 'After all, there are very few wines here that really express the terroir's potential to its maximum. So many factors get in the way, from new oak to international grape varieties. I felt something truly Friulan was missing. In the Loire I saw that the vieilles vignes wines showed more salinity, minerality and depth. I was also interested in making a white wine for ageing, and only old vines offered that possibility. So I was led to work with old vines *per forza*, by necessity.'

We visited some of the vineyards. In one case, a single hill was divided between past and current cultivation systems. The difference was visibly striking: Perco's grassy, sloping vineyard followed the curves of the hill and looked green and lush; on the other side, his neighbour's slope had been carved into flat stepped terraces favoured by mechanization, was browned from weedkillers, and its vineyards looked forced and unnatural. 'Of course it costs far more to maintain the vineyards as I do, working completely manually, so it's only by producing an important wine here that I can afford to do this,' he explains.

Not all old vines are worth keeping. Marco Perco has studied the sites and their fruit carefully before deciding which of them give the best results. His list of wines includes single-variety Pinot Bianco, Sauvignon and Tocai Friulano, as well as the red Val di Miez, of Merlot and Cabernet Franc. All the wines are aged slowly and are released after a minimum of 18 months. Vecchie Vigne comes out after three years and even then is only just beginning to express its complexity. Its life expectancy is much longer, as vertical tastings going back to the first year, 1999, show. The 2004, tasted in 2008, is the result of a blend from eight vineyards, all aged over 40 years. Of 70 percent Malvasia, it is striking for the minerality and salinity that leave the palate energized and wanting more, and for the elegance that it expresses despite its age. It's a wine, like so many of Marco Perco's, that will keep gaining character through time and will fully repay whatever attention and respect we are willing to give it, much like a patient conversation with a wise elder.

Casa Griunit is the Perco family's agriturismo, located in a converted stable building above the meeting rooms of the winery. The four mini apartments are decorated in eclectic style, and continue the young artsy atmosphere of Roncùs. The rooms overlook the garden and vineyards, and offer a personalized, relaxed base from which to discover the Collio's charms.

Wine, Agriturismo

Via Russiz, 7
Capriva del Friuli
TEL 0481 99164
www.marcofelluga.it

Russiz Superiore

This estate, long in the family of Marco Felluga (see p. 223 for his other estate at Gradisca d'Isonzo), is one of the most historic of the Collio wineries. Today it is run by Roberto Felluga, Marco's son. I love to visit Russiz Superiore, with its beautiful old villa perched on top of the hill commanding views that stretch all the way across the valley of Preval to the Slovenian mountains. It's surrounded by gardens and by vineyards that seem like extensions of those gardens. Just below the house sit the imposing cellar buildings, which combine an atmospheric sense of history with the latest technology for making wines. From this 50-hectare estate, Roberto Felluga produces his top line named, appropriately enough, Russiz Superiore. It's the closest the Collio comes to a château, growing all its own grapes and working only the best selections for this label.

Roberto Felluga is a generous, genial man whose life has been shaped by growing up in one of the area's leading wine families. Like his father, he's a firm believer in the Collio and its unique qualities. 'The image we must present of the Collio is of a place with a special vocation for white wines,' he says. 'Even if the reds made here are excellent too. But it's the whites which have changed so remarkably in the last twenty years as we have radically reduced the amount of grapes being produced by each vine. That has really made the terroir express itself in the wines. And that distinguishes our wines in the Collio from every other Italian winemaking region. We Friulani are very hard workers, and I'm proud of how first my father's and now my generation have been able to make such a difference to this area.' The

Marco and Roberto Felluga

Opposite: The view from the vineyards of Russiz towards the Slovenian hills

The cellars at Russiz Superiore

Collio Bianco Col Disôre Russiz Superiore is a blend of Pinot Bianco, Friulano, Sauvignon and Ribolla Giallo vinified in large wooden barrels.

With his wife, Elena Marocchi, Roberto has recently launched into another project at Russiz Superiore, a deluxe agriturismo which is scheduled to open in 2009.

Wine

Schiopetto

Via Palazzo Arcivescovile, 1
Capriva del Friuli
TEL 0481 80332
www.schiopetto.it

As I've travelled up and down the Collio interviewing wine producers for this book, one person has been named repeatedly as the inspiration for not only the current generation of winemakers but also for their fathers: Mario Schiopetto. Sadly he died in 2003, before my first visit to the Collio, so I never had the pleasure of meeting him, but I have visited his beautiful estate, tasted his great wines and met his children.

'Mario was considered one of the fathers of Friuli's white wines,' says Carlo Schiopetto who, with his twin brother, Giorgio, and sister, Maria Angela, now runs the historic winery at Capriva. 'Ninety percent of our wines are still white. You could say we work on the idea of moving forwards while keeping an eye to the past.'

Mario Schiopetto's role in helping to launch Friuli's quality viticulture can't be overestimated. He began making white wines using low temperatures as early as 1969; did his first vinification experiments without the use of sulphur dioxide in the early '70s, and instilled a culture of excellence in the vineyards that still inspires today. Mario Schiopetto was befriended and championed by Luigi Veronelli, Italy's first and foremost wine critic in an era when Italy was still trying to prove it had a national viticulture. He won prizes and set standards, all with a clear vision of wine as pure expression of its grapes, with nothing added to distract from that. His historic Blanc des Rosis blend first came out in 1986, a blend of Tocai, Pinot Bianco, Sauvignon and Malvasia. Today, it includes a little Ribolla, and is still a prize-winner.

The credo of making white wines that could last well in time without the need for barrel ageing is still followed by many today; Schiopetto himself began using some wood for selected whites in 1994, but this didn't change the basic message of purity, cleanliness and finesse.

'We don't de-stalk our white grapes, but working very quickly so as to obviate the use of sulphites, we press them softly before using gravity to separate the must from the rest,' says Carlo. The Schiopettos are now assisted in the vineyards by Marco Simonit. The young team have catalogued and analyzed each of the estate's 32 hectares of vineyards, and reduced the number of wines being made to eight: six whites and two reds.

The Schiopettos have a dynamic approach to Friuli's future for winemaking: 'We'd like to open out to the world more,' says Carlo. 'This is such a great place for wine and yet so few people know it. There's a lot more work to be done, but we're ready to take it on!'

The Schiopetto brothers, Carlo and Giorgio

Wine, Hotel, Golf Club, Restaurant
Castello di Spessa – Pali Wines

Via Spessa, 1
Capriva del Friuli
TEL 0481 60445
www.paliwines.com

A magnificent avenue of lofty horse chestnuts leads up to the castle of Spessa, planted after the war by the Americans. The nucleus of the Castello's historic buildings date from 1200, and were probably built on a Longobard site chosen for its excellent views of the plains and, in the distance, the sea. The neo-Gothic castle we see today was designed by Ruggero Berlam and built at the beginning of the 20th century. It's surrounded by a well-kept park, with romantic wisteria and rose arbours. In the course of its long history the Castello has housed generations of noble families – Casanova was a visitor in 1773 – and was even used as superior billets by the Germans in the Second World War. An 18-hole golf course set amongst the vineyards now extends beyond these central buildings, with a handsome club-house and Tavernetta restaurant at the foot of the hill beneath them. For the last six years, the Castello has been run as a luxury hotel, but it also houses neat rows of barriques in its long, vaulted underground cellars; they are unique in scale in the Collio.

Above: The Castello di
Spessa from the rose
arbour

The Castello's owner, Loretto Pali, is an industrialist from the field of furniture-making; he specializes in children's furniture and is a leader in his sector. His winery, Pali Wines, produces grapes from 30 hectares of vineyards in the Collio, of which 22 are at Capriva, and the remainder in Cormòns. The winery's output is of circa 100,000 bottles per year, of which 80% are whites. Currently, Loretto Pali is working with œnologists Gianni Menotti (see below) as the external consultant and Domenico Lovat, who is the resident winemaker; they are aided by Marco Simonit's team of agronomists. Paolo della Rovere is the commercial director. This team also manages Pali's second winery, La Boatina, nearby in the Isonzo DOC close to Cormòns.

As early as the 1970s Pali also became interested in wine tourism, and began developing this ambitious project. Work began in 1988 to restructure the estate, and lasted until 2000 when it was officially opened. The hotel now offers fifteen luxurious rooms, sumptuously furnished in 18th-century style, with ten more above the Tavernetta. This beautiful and perfectly kept resort offers a unique oasis from which to visit the vineyards of the Collio, the nearby seaside at Grado, or the mountains.

Wine

Via Russiz, 6
Capriva del Friuli
TEL 0481 80047
www.villarussiz.it

Villa Russiz

Villa Russiz is a model winery. Not just because it's beautiful and beautifully kept. Nor because it makes great wines, though it does. I know I'm not alone in admiring it also for its social commitment. Villa Russiz is a rare example of a publicly-owned winery whose proceeds go to sustain a charity set up over a century ago.

In 1869, when Count Théodore de La Tour married an Austrian noblewoman, Elvine von Ritter Zahony, they received 100 hectares of land in the Collio as a wedding present from her family. He was a Frenchman from Graz. As a connoisseur of European wines and viticulture, he was confident that French grape varieties would grow well there. De La Tour became one of the first to import Chardonnay, Sauvignon, Cabernet Sauvignon and the Pinots Bianco and Grigio into Friuli. 'Now, 150 years later, I think we can safely claim them as our own,' says Gianni Menotti, the award-winning winemaker who, for many years, has been making Villa Russiz' wines. 'This area was under Austrian rule then and the countryside was given over to small farms and rustic agriculture. De La Tour built the castle and the cellar at Villa Russiz, and brought in all-important œnological know-how,' Menotti explains as we tour the historic ageing cellars under the landmark white castle.

The noble couple had no children, but Elvine began to take in babies and small children from the surrounding peasant families, feeding and schooling them in a precursor to a modern

The de La Tour mausoleum

day-care centre. By the time her husband died in 1894 she was caring for over 40 childen. After the First World War, Elvine de La Tour was being helped with the children by another exceptional woman, Countess Adele Cerruti, known locally as Suor Adele, Sister Adele who, in 1919 founded an institute for war orphans. When Elvine decided to return to Austria, she left Villa Russiz to the Austrian government, who passed it over to the Italians, where it became the Elvine de La Tour Foundation. Today, under the guidance of Silvano Stefanutti, Villa Russiz is what the Italians call *un ente morale,* or charity, under the auspices of Istituto Adele Cerruti; it currently aids about twenty local children in need.

Gianni Menotti's father, Edino, himself a skilled winemaker, joined Villa Russiz in 1954, wanting to contribute to the cause. He stayed for 35 years, bringing his son into the fold in 1988. 'I studied agriculture and joined my father here,' says Gianni Menotti. 'There was so much to do and I felt so small compared to some of the great wineries that were all around us!' In 1988 he began to make big changes in the 35 hectares of vineyards, reducing yields and improving work in the cellar. In the vineyards he works closely with Giordano Figheli, a councillor in the Collio's Consortium. The results have not been slow in coming. The wines started winning prizes in Italy and beyond; in 2006, Gianni Menotti was named winemaker of the year by Gambero Rosso-Slow Food.

Of the wines, Chardonnay Gräfin de La Tour has been awarded best Italian white wine; Sauvignon de La Tour too has become an icon: a harmonious balance of floral aromas and structure whose fine acidity gives it length and class. Menotti's work with Friulano has also been successful: vinified exclusively in steel, the wine remains luminous and fresh, with clean varietal character. Other classics include Graf de La Tour Merlot and Collio Malvasia and Pinot Bianco.

OTHER WINERIES
Ronco Blanchis
Blanchis 70, Mossa ; Tel. 0481 80519
Budignac – Daniele Tonut
Via Zorutti 114, Capriva Del Friuli; tel 0481 808663
Vidussi Gestioni Agricole
Spessa 18, 34070 Capriva Del Friuli; tel 0481 80072
Daniele Grion
Via Garibaldi 4, Capriva del Friuli; tel 0481 808660

Opposite: Gianni Menotti

Chapter 3

Cormòns
and its hills

From Pradis via Subida, Novali, Plessiva and Zegla to Brazzano

The town of Cormòns is the effective centre of the Collio wine-making district. From here the roads lead in all directions into the vineyard areas, each with their own characteristics and microclimates. They are famous for Pinot Bianco and especially for Tocai Friulano, which in the best sites attains great minerality and an unmistakable, faintly almondy aftertaste. This large chapter begins with the town of Cormòns and the wineries to its south and west; it then goes south-east to Pradis; north-east to Subida and the crus of Novali, Plessiva and Zegla; and north to Brazzano. Cormòns is a must for anyone interested in the Collio, and fun to visit as it also hosts several colourful festivals each year (see pP. 41-42).

Cormòns

The picturesque small town of Cormòns sits in the valley below the steep hillside of Monte Quarin which, at 274 metres above sea level, commands views across the Isonzo plain to the sea. On top of it are the remains of a fortified castle that was built by the patriarchs of Aquileia in the 11th century as a sanctuary when they withdrew from their base in the coastal flatlands for fear of attack. (The castle was destroyed in 1508 by the Venetian general D'Alviano). In the 13th century, Cormòns came under the auspices of the Ghibelline counts of Gorizia, for whom it was a key feudal stronghold. Cormòns was at the centre of a long war between the Venetian army and the Hapsburgs; it became part of the Austro-Hungarian Empire after the Diet of Worms in 1521. From then until 1918 it

Opposite: A sculptural old vine on Monte Quarin, above Cormòns

The view of Cormòns from Monte Quarin, with the Adriatic Sea in the distance

remained under Hapsburg rule, with the brief exception of a few years when Napoleonic troops took power; from 1866 it acted as an important station along the border between Italy and the Austrian Empire.

Cormòns' medieval town plan, built in concentric double circles around the Duomo, was renewed in the baroque era, as several church facades can testify. Cormòns was always an important agricultural hub. In 1860, with the completion of the railway line that linked Udine to Trieste, and that joined the existing line from Trieste to Vienna, Cormòns' wines and fresh fruits could be delivered in record time to the northern Hapsburg cities. The annual cherry market took over the town's central piazzas, with row upon row of large baskets filled with the sweet fruits. There were weekly and monthly markets selling livestock, barrels, wine, silk cocoons, game, grain, flowers and vegetables.

Each year, in August, a fair called Rievocazione Storica celebrates the town's medieval heritage with costumes, artisan

trades, and the re-enactment of court tournaments. Today
Cormòns is the heart of the Collio: it houses the headquarters
of the Consortium, and offers a central point from which
to explore the several well-signposted wine roads into the
Collio hills.

EATING AND DRINKING IN CORMÒNS

Artisan Producer: Prosciutto

Lorenzo D'Osvaldo

Via Dante, 40
Cormòns
TEL 0481 61644

Ask anyone in the Collio, in Friuli or beyond, who makes the
most special *prosciutti* of them all, and the answer invariably
comes back: Lorenzo D'Osvaldo. This brilliant artisan is alone
in carrying on a tradition begun by his father 65 years ago. In a
large historic villa on a hillside in central Cormòns, D'Osvaldo
hand-picks, salts and cures locally reared hams before giving
them a light smoking in a purpose-built smokehouse behind the
villa. In it, a fire is lit of cherry, bay and rosemary woods for the
smoke. A large copper cauldron in the smokehouse is filled with
water and herbs to maintain humidity and aromatic flavour.
The hams, complete with trotter, are then aged for from 12 to
26 months hanging in large rooms on the top floor of the villa,
with windows back and front that D'Osvaldo opens by hand,
allowing the chill winter breeze to enter as necessary to keep the
temperatures constant.

'Salting and smoking together form the oldest way to sterilize
a food, in the equivalent of long, slow boiling,' explains
Lorenzo. The result is a prosciutto that tastes very subtly of
smoke, very subtly of salt, and that is given an added dimension
by the herbs. It's all done by touch and experience: D'Osvaldo
knows instinctively how to protect the prosciutti from extremes
of temperature. The D'Osvaldo hams and Speck are some of
Italy's most sought-after foods and are sold in the country's best
shops and restaurants; he can never keep up with the demand
for them.

Sounds like a perfect story, doesn't it? Sadly, Lorenzo
D'Osvaldo's *prosciuttificio* is currently at the centre of a bureau-
cratic row that involves Brussels, Rome and the local Friulian
authorities, who have ordered him to stop work. They claim
that his way of curing the hams is breaking EU hygiene norms
introduced to safeguard industrial food processing. No one is
questioning the safety levels of D'Osvaldo's hams; they have
been tested and found to be completely in line with the regula-
tions. Rather, it is the small details of the artisan curing process
that have come under attack: for instance, the smokeroom

*Opposite: Lorenzo
D'Osvaldo with one of
his prize hams*

should, by law, be tiled. D'Osvaldo maintains that his system, in which the walls are painted with the natural lime that has always been used in this tradition, absorbs more humidity and allows the walls to breathe rather than sweat. The same is true of the cooling rooms: the legislators want computer-controlled refrigeration instead of D'Osvaldo's instinctive method. 'The difficulty in being a lone artisan working in this way is that I have no group or lobby to defend me,' he says. His cause has been picked up by the media but as yet no solution has been found. In the meantime, D'Osvaldo continues to cure some hams at a nearby friend's factory. But, he says, the results just are not the same. Let's hope he wins his fight or the world will have lost one more of its precious and unique hand-made foods.

Bakery

Via Gorizia, 7
TEL 0481 630664
www.chiarosa.it

Pasticceria Panetteria Bonelli

This old-fashioned bakery and pastry shop faces the statue of Maximilian I, the Hapsburg emperor, in Piazza della Libertà. You can't miss its red wine-coloured shutters and painted door. Inside, the quaint shop is full of delicious treats. There are assorted breads and rolls, but it's for the cookies that Bonelli is justly famous. They're uniquely Friulian in name and flavour: Friulini (round, short-pastry); Zimui ('twin' chocolate and vanilla rounds); Claps (dusted with icing sugar and sold in wonderful round tins); and the enigmatic Ricetta 101, crunchy-soft biscuits designed to go with wine. They make great presents, if you can keep from eating them all yourself on the way home.

Food Shop

Via Cumano, 5
Cormòns
TEL 0481 61305

Alimentari Tomadin

This charming grocery shop sells all the best local and Friulian specialities. Marisa Tomadin and her daughter, Leila, have assembled a very personal collection, from D'Osvaldo's fabulous lightly smoked prosciutto to Zoff's cheeses, from flours for making pasta to the maize and other grain products of La Blave di Mortean cooperative. Here you can find polenta flours and rice, fruit jams and wine jellies... a gastronomic treasure trove.

Hotel, Restaurant

Via San Giovanni, 45
Cormòns
TEL 0481 60214
www.hotelfelcaro.it

Hotel Felcaro

This is the best place to stay if you want to be in Cormòns itself. The family run hotel, situated in an Austrian villa, is surrounded by gardens and offers a swimming pool and tennis courts. From here it's easy to go for lovely walks up Monte Quarin or into town for a drink or shopping. Rooms are

divided between the villa, where they are decorated with antique
style furniture, and the new annexes, which offer more modern
accomodation. The restaurant, which features game as a speciality, also offers a good cellar of Collio wines, in addition to the
family's own production.

Restaurant, Café, Pastries, Hotel

Al Giardinetto

Via Matteotti, 54
Cormòns
TEL 0481 60257
www.jre.it
CLOSED Mon, Tues
PRICE €€€€

This is one of the most established restaurants in the Collio. It's
situated right in the centre of town, in a period house with a
garden terrace. Beyond the dining rooms is a lovely pasticceria-
bar where you can get snacks, coffees and drinks all day.
There are also three rooms for guests wishing to stay in
Cormòns. The restaurant's chef and owner, Paolo Zoppolatti, is
the third generation of his family to run Trattoria Il Giardinetto,
'the little garden', and has long been a member of the Jeunes
Restaurateurs d'Europe. As for the food, it runs a course
between traditional and creative styles. In autumn, sausage-
meatballs are served with polenta; *blek*, the local rough-shaped
pasta squares, come with clams, mussels and a green broccoli
sauce; pasta is rolled around a pumpkin-walnut filling and
served with a strong cheese sauce. *Cervo*, or venison, comes
cubed and cooked with vegetables in a Kilner jar, accompanied
by creamy polenta. Well-made, rich desserts finish the meal. The
wine list is filled with treats from the Collio and surrounding
areas, and offers a small daily list of wines by the glass.

Wine Bar

Enoteca di Cormòns

Piazza XXIV Maggio, 21
Cormòns
OPEN 11.00 to 22.00;
CLOSED Tuesday
PRICE €€

If Cormòns is the heart of the Collio, the Enoteca is the heart of
Cormòns. It's situated in the town's grand central piazza, in one
wing of 18th-century Palazzo Locatelli, the elegant town hall.
The Enoteca's tables spill out into the piazza in summer, by the
cooling modern fountain that is a focal point of the long, rec-
tangular square. The Enoteca is run as a co-operative, with 33
members who are among the top wine producers of the Collio
and Isonzo. It was founded in 1990 in order to promote the
area's best wine and food; it also acts as one of the town's
tourist information points, and hosts tastings, exhibitions and
lectures. Most of all, it's a fun, lively place to hang out. In the
evenings, the winemaker members are often present, relaxing
after a day in the cellars or vineyards, exchanging ideas and
tasting each other's wines. You can buy wines by the glass or
bottle, accompanied by platters of D'Osvaldo prosciutto or
other local *salumi* and cheeses. It's open all day, so it's a great
place for a mid-morning or afternoon snack, or aperitivo.

*Cormòns street with
Monte Quarin behind*

Artisan Producer: Meat

Macello Comunale di Cormòns

Via Corona, 14
Cormòns
TEL 335 718884
www.norcinicormons
.com

Until recently the figure of the *norcino* was of crucial importance throughout rural Italy. It was he who slaughtered the pigs
that every country household kept in a small lean-to behind the
barn. All through the winter, when the temperatures were low
enough to stop the meat from going bad (in pre-refrigeration
times) families would book the services of their local *norcino* to
come on an appointed day to kill the pig they had lovingly fattened for a year in preparation for this great event. Every part
of the pig's body was precious, from its fat to its feet. The families would organize themselves with friends and relatives so as
to make light of the many jobs at hand: butchering the carcass,
carefully salting the hind quarters for prosciutto, grinding or
chopping smaller cuts of meat for *salame*, *ossocollo* and the infinite other salt-cured meats the pork could be turned into. Even

the blood was caught and made into sausages. There was wine and a great mood of celebration and thanksgiving for this unique source of protein that, if carefully preserved, could last for a full year.

With changes in agriculture and urban zoning in recent years, it has become increasingly difficult for the *norcino* to practise his craft, just as it has become harder to obtain permission to rear the pigs. I was fascinated to discover that many of the winemaking families in the Collio do still rear one or two pigs for home use. (The pigs are a perfect way of recycling leftover foods.) The problem remains how to legally butcher them.

Cormòns' Comune has sponsored an excellent initiative, with help from councillor Renato Toros: it has restructured the town slaughterhouse, built in 1872, which fell into disuse in 1992. The building has been modernized and is now ready to be used for butchering pigs being raised by local families. The Cooperativa Norcini del Collio & Isonzo di Cormòns, a group of professionally trained butchers, young and old, now operate at the Macello, and help keep this important gastronomic culture alive.

Artisan Producer: Cheese
Giuseppe and Patrizia Zoff

Via Parini, 18
Borgnano di Cormòns
TEL 0481 67204
www.borgdaocjs.it
DAIRY OPEN FOR
PURCHASES Mon-Sat
8–12, 15-18.30

A five-minute drive south-west from Cormòns towards Medea, and you come to the village of Borgnano. Until a few decades ago, this was all open farmland punctuated by a few houses or barns. Recent building has cut into the fields but at the heart of Borgnano, a tree-lined drive brings you into one place that seems to have remained unchanged: the Zoff's dairy. Giuseppe Zoff is a wonderful character. The day I last visited he had just helped in the birthing of a calf, always an important event on a dairy farm.

'We have sixty cows in our herd, of which about half are giving milk at any one time,' he explains. The animals are kept in spacious stables with access to an outdoor yard. 'It's a sad fact, but over 70 percent of Italy's small farms have closed in the last twenty years. We're determined to keep going though, even if it means taking ten steps backwards to get there. It's no good feeding our animals with hay or grain that has been doused in chemicals and then expect them to remain healthy.' Zoff grows 90 percent of his herd's feed himself, without the use of chemical fertilizers or pesticides. 'Italy's future is in its *prodotti tipici*, or artisan products, along with tourism and agriculture, but if we are not helped by our government and the EU to maintain what is special about hand-made foods, we'll just be giving in to the pressures of industry.'

Opposite: Giuseppe Zoff with two of his cheeses

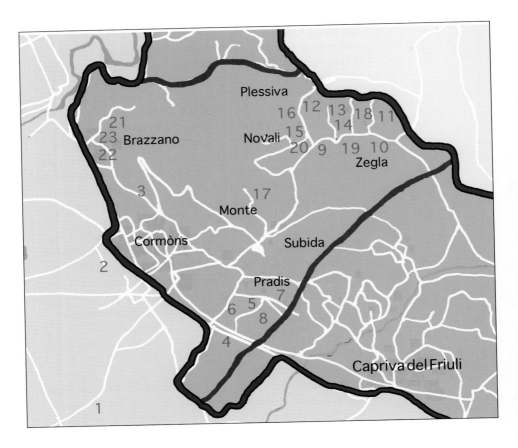

Zoff's delicious cheeses are made by his wife, Patrizia, using unpasteurized milk from their Friuli Pezzata Rossa cows. 'The locals love our products. We can't keep up with demand,' he says. His products include yoghurt, which is made using milk heated to 70°C, and a number of interesting cheeses. Latteria Friulana is a semi-cooked round cheese best aged for sixty days, but usually sold after thirty as it is so popular; for the *caciotto aromatizzato*, the milk is only heated to body temperature before being infused with nettles, rosemary or other herbs. *Ricotta al forno* is baked with a little olive oil in a basket mould; it retains a delicate acidity and the sweet flavour of fresh milk.

Cormòns Wineries

These wineries all have their cellars and headquarters in the mostly flat lands to the west of Cormòns; many of their vineyards are, however, situated in higher positions in the Collio hills.

Wine

Angoris

Angoris, 7 Cormòns
TEL 0481 60923
www.angoris.com

As you approach Cormòns from Medea, you can't help but notice a long line of lofty cypress trees on the valley floor as Cormòns comes into sight. Get closer, and it reveals itself to be a cypress avenue so imposing that it is only beaten by the world-famous one in Bolgheri, Tuscany, which has inspired poets for generations. Cormòns' cypress avenue belongs to the Angoris winery.

This sizeable estate's managing director is Claudia Locatelli, the daughter of the owner, Luciano Locatelli. She runs the business with winemaker Alessandro Dal Zovo. No mean feat for two such young people, given the size of the property: 630 hectares in all, of which 130 are vineyards divided between three DOCs. From these, Angoris produces a large catalogue of wines.

Dal Zovo explained the strategy for their new vineyards in the Isonzo plain: 'With so many hectares, we've been replanting using the French model of more plants per hectare, each producing less fruit. This enables us to use machines to do a lot of the work while cutting down on petrol and chemicals, as more grapes are produced within a smaller amount of space.' Within the Collio DOC, the estate has ten hectares at Ruttars, between Cormòns and Dolegna. These are on the hillsides, so a different strategy applies: here, grape varieties are selected following geological studies. Once the grapes arrive in the spacious cellars, selected yeasts are used, as is micro-oxygenation to replace the

The cypress avenue
at Angoris

work of barrels. Of the Collio wines, Pinot Grigio, Friulano and Chardonnay are worked exclusively in steel, using yields of 50 to 60 quintals of grapes per hectare, with 24-hour macerations inside the presses for the two white varieties before soft pressing.

Claudia Locatelli explained more about the history of the estate: 'My grandfather bought it at auction in 1968 from a count who had gone bankrupt,' she says. 'In 1970 he built a big cellar, and the family involvement here was launched.' Her father is an industrialist, and runs other kinds of manufacturing businesses, so Claudia is now the third generation to handle Angoris. In 1993, when she arrived, she was very young and was put to work in every department of the winemaking business. 'After a number of years of working just to produce high numbers, I've finally been able to make the family realize that only through investing in quality can we make wines that will speak of this territory, the wines I've always dreamed of – and at the right price!'

Claudia Locatelli and
Alessandro Dal Zovo in
front of the Angoris villa

Angoris' imposing 16th-century villa is currently used for private guests only, but there is a lovely shop beside the cellar for direct sales and cellar visits.

Wine
Drius

Via Filanda, 100
Cormòns
TEL 0481 60998
drius.mauro@adriacom.it

Mauro Drius lives across the road from his cellar, just south of the Cormòns railway line. The house is flanked by the vineyards and fields which dominate this important agricultural plain. Drius lives here with his parents, wife, Nadia, and three children. Mauro grew up helping his parents run the farm which then had small fields of crops and orchards, a few animals and some vineyards. Over time they converted from this mixed culture to the single pursuit of vine-growing. 'In the '60s and early

'70s, when my grandfather and father were planting vines, they followed the fashion of their day leaving wide rows and spaces between the vines,' Drius says. 'Now our new vineyards are planted much more tightly, with up to 5,500 plants per hectare, and are trained to Guyot.'

As is the case in many other Collio estates, the Drius vineyards are not all in one place, but are located several hundred metres apart. Of their 14 hectares of vineyards, 2.2 are in the DOC Collio, including some on the south-west hillside of Mt Quarin above Brazzano which favours Tocai Friulano; the rest are in the Isonzo DOC, in the limestone flats of the valley that are best for the Pinots Bianco and Grigio. Their total output is of 70,000 bottles, of which 8,000 are in the Collio DOC, but they have plans to double that to 16,000 over the next few years. Most of their wines – 85% – are whites, and of those, most are worked in stainless steel. 'I'm not in favour of maceration for these grape varieties,' says Drius. 'I like my wines to be drinkable and retain their *'freschezza'*. I also like them to be single-variety, so that I can taste and clearly appreciate one grape type at a time.' Whole grapes are pressed softly; the must is cooled to between 13° and 16°C to stop it fermenting for the first 12 hours, then selected natural yeasts are added. 'Selected yeasts enable us to reduce our use of sulphites,' he explains. 'We rack immediately, to protect the wine from oxidizing and bottle in April, adding a little sulphite to protect the wines.' His clean, drinkable Collio Sauvignon and Tocai Friulano are representative of this approach.

'The Collio contains many microclimates and types of terrain so it's up to each producer to create their own individual identity, to make their mark on the territory,' says Drius, a lanky, soft-spoken man in his late forties. 'For example, here near the plain it's always a few degrees warmer than up in the hills, so you have to choose your varieties accordingly. As a producer you have to make decisions too about how to manage the vineyards. Our approach is to work partly organically and partly using more modern products: we're trying to reduce the chemical impact on the land, using minimal quantities and modern tractors that can save petrol and drastically reduce wasted chemicals, by recycling them. But in a year like 2008, there has been so much rain that if we had stuck solely to organic methods we wouldn't have had a grape left in the vineyards. I think you have to be pragmatic, to interpret each year as it comes.'

As Mauro and I were sitting talking outside in early August, his father came by with several vegetable seed packets in his hand. 'What's he doing with seeds at this time of year?' I asked.

Mauro Drius

'My father plants vegetables in every open space he finds around our property,' he replied, shaking his head and smiling. 'That's the thing about that generation of *contadini:* they know what it means to go hungry, so even though we've got plenty to eat now, he never stops growing more.' Luckily, some old habits die hard.

Wine

Raccaro

Via San Giovanni, 87
Cormòns
TEL 0481 61425
az.agr.raccaro@alice.it

Dario Raccaro is a central figure in Collio life, not only because he makes such distinctive wines, but also because he is the president of the Enoteca di Cormòns (see p. 130). When he's not working in the vineyards, he can often be found at one end of the Piazza XXIV Maggio or the other: organizing tastings and keeping an eye on supplies at the Enoteca, or sitting on the veranda of the Bar Rullo with his winemaking chums, catching up on all the latest grapevine news.

Raccaro's grandfather bought the property in 1928, one year after coming back from working as a miner in the US. 'He found a stone house and a *ronco* – a hill – with two hectares of land,' says Dario. 'In those days the Cormòn Collio vines were all here, on the slopes of Monte Quarin, up at Pradis and a bit in Capriva. The fertile plain was best suited to crops, so the vines were planted where nothing else would grow, on the hillsides. This has always been *una terra da vino.*' Vines were found to be more lucrative than other crops, so the Raccaros gradually converted all their property to vineyards.

'The old folk here recounted that one particular plot, called Rolat, was known to be the best location for Tocai,' says Raccaro. 'It's just up behind the small church of Santa Maria in Apollonia, a few hundred metres from our house. This terraced vineyard was originally planted in 1898, and subsequently replanted using cuttings from those first vines.' Raccaro makes a Tocai Friulano called Vigna del Rolat, a wine that retains its fruit with notes of green apples and dandelion, then opens out with natural energy into a salty, softly bitter finish. Raccaro is a purist, and favours whites made without the use of wood or maceration. His clean Malvasia is another demonstration of this: a lightly aromatic, mineral, long wine that marries well with fish and has the 'sprint' to age well for a few years. 'Recently there's been a change in consumers' tastes away from the highly charged international varieties towards more subtle wines – and that suits us well as that's always been our style. Malvasia Istriana used to be a "forgotten" variety, now it's even fashionable with the Japanese.'

Opposite: Vineyards below the church at Brazzano

Dario, Dalila, Paolo Raccaro and their dog

Dario works the vines and wines with his son, Paolo, and wife, Dalila; his second son, Luca, is studying œnology too. The family's annual production is of around 35,000 bottles from 4.5 hectares, of which 2.5 are rented. As well as the whites (their Collio Bianco is a blend of Tocai Friulano, Sauvignon and Pinot Grigio, with a pinch of two other whites), the Raccaros also produce a fruity, elegant Merlot from a vineyard that rises up behind the house. 'Small, family estates like ours have to make wines of character to compete with the bigger, industrial producers who can dominate prices in the markets,' says Dario. 'We are able to invest more energy in the vineyards than they can, and work our high quality grapes more naturally. That's our strong point.'

Wine

Via Isonzo, 135
Cormòns
TEL 0481 60446
www.venturinivini.it

Paolo Venturini

There's a breeze up on the gentle hillside where Paolo Venturini has recently planted his new vineyards, in a sloping amphitheatre south of the railway near Cormòns. From here you can see the higher hill of Pradis, with the Slovenian mountains behind it. 'Originally, when the Collio was first formed, in 1964, its lower boundary was drawn along that train line; later tests proved that two other hills south of that line had the same geological structure – the *ponca* – and similar microclimates to the rest of the Collio so, when the first *disciplinare* was drawn up, in 1968, the boundaries were enlarged to include them,' says this dapper businessman who has recently given himself over to making wines. It's quite unusual in the Collio to find such a large block of vines belonging to a single owner. 'My family,

who run the brick factory, Vecchia Fornace di Laterizi, bought
the first six hectares of vineyards here in the late 1940s. Over
the last six years we've increased those to eighteen: twelve in the
Collio hills and six in the Isonzo plain.' Venturini is
particularly proud of the ten hectares he's replanted here, of primarily Sauvignon and Ribolla Gialla vines; Pinot Grigio will be
added in the next round of plantings. 'I wanted to concentrate
my energies and investments on redoing the vineyards before
tackling the building of a new cellar,' he says. Work on the cellar will begin in 2009 or 2010.

Above the amphitheatre is a small, sloping vineyard with
crooked old vines and a few fruit trees around it. 'This vineyard
will not be ripped out: it's one of our most important assets, for
it contains a rich assortment of white grape varieties, some of
which are now very rare here,' he explains.

A short ride in the Jeep takes us to Venturini's two hectares
of vineyards at Pradis, one of the Collio's most sought-after
terroirs. The Venturini family planted these in the 1960s,
favouring Pinot Bianco and Tocai Friulano here. 'The soils of
Pradis give great results with these varieties. Indeed, I bottle this
Pinot Bianco by itself.' As we tour the vineyards, I notice that
they are weedkiller-free. 'I'd never use it in any of my vineyards,' he says. 'In fact, at Pradis, very few people do. For me
it's a contradiction in terms to say you respect your vineyard and
then use those products.' Venturini is helped in the vineyards by

Paolo Venturini in his
vineyards near Cormòns

Gianni Menotti, Villa Russiz's talented young winemaker.
Venturini favours a clean style in his wines. He is particularly
proud of the Pinot Bianco, Tocai Friulano and Malvasia Istriana
wines he produces in the Collio. 'I've only begun making quality
wines in the last six years,' he says, 'so for me this is an exciting
work in progress.'

Pradis

The Regina dei Vigneti

This small area of gently sloping hills was once given over mostly to fields, with cherry orchards and some vines. In recent
decades the vines have been given priority. At Pradis the temperatures are a little higher than elsewhere in the Collio, as the hills
face south and are protected from the cold winds from the
north and east. This helps explain why this great cru of *flysh*
is known for the richness and structure it offers to its wines,
especially to Pinot Bianco, Malvasia, Tocai Friulano and
Chardonnay. Pradis is easily identifiable for its iconic protector
who is housed in a tiny chapel that dominates the vineyards: *la
Regina dei Vigneti*, or Queen of the Vines. Every year, on March
19th, the residents of Pradis take her out to celebrate the *festa
di San Giuseppe*, before returning her safely to her shrine for
another year.

Wine
Paolo Caccese

Pradis, 6
Cormòns
TEL 0481 61062
www.paolocaccese.it

Paolo Caccese is a lawyer turned winemaker and his small,
model cellar sits on a hilltop at Pradis, one of the Collio's most
sought-after crus. 'My father, who was an engineer with origins
in Campania, bought this simple stone house with two hectares
of vineyards around it in 1954,' says Caccese. 'What started as
a hobby – to make over the house and produce a bit of wine –
became a more serious passion for me,' he says. In 1988 he was
offered another three and a half hectares in the area, bringing
his total up to six. 'When I started out these vines were jungles,'
he says, shaking his head. 'Yet the fifteen years from 1975 to
1990 were amazing for those of us in the Collio who were making good wines. We easily sold everything both abroad and in
Italy. Ours was the first area in Friuli really to produce wines of
quality with a recognizable provenance – thanks to pioneers like
Attems and Schiopetto.'

In 1964 the Consortium was born. Caccese has been on its
council for 25 years; he also served as its president for a one-
year period; he left to be able to dedicate more time to his
wines. If things are more competitive now for the Collio in a

*Paolo Caccese looks
out over his vineyards
at Pradis*

globalized wine market, Caccese feels its best strategy is to go
on producing wines of high quality, niche wines. 'That's the only
way we can justify the prices our wines cost us to make. In
today's world, working manually in hillside vineyards is exorbi-
tantly expensive. After all, the Collio's total output is of just
seven million bottles from 1500 hectares of registered vineyards,' he says. That's less than the Gallo family alone. Here the
average estate is of 13 hectares, which means that many are

*Malvasia Istriana
vineyards at Caccese
before the harvest*

Paolo Caccese

very much smaller than that. We have to make that a feature, not a handicap.'

Paolo Caccese, whose PR is handled by Veronica Caccese, makes a sizeable list of wines: eight whites, three reds and one dessert wine. 'All my wines are single-varietal as I feel it's difficult to imagine that one wine, the Collio Bianco blend, could ever really represent the Collio's complexity. I prefer to maintain each variety's unique identity.' Caccese is known for his clean drinkable wines that reflect the minerality of their terroir. One of his favourites is the Malvasia which, like Pinot Bianco, does so well in the terroir of Pradis.

Wine

Carlo di Pradis

Pradis, 22
Cormòns
TEL 0481 62272
www.carlodipradis.it

Many Collio estates have undergone a recent generational change as fathers pass the reins to their sons and daughters. 'This switch hasn't been easy for some of our friends,' says David Buzzinelli who, with his older brother Boris, took over the running of the family winery in 1992. 'But in our case it went very smoothly. We were lucky that our father, Carlo, gave us carte blanche.'

'He would grumble that we were crazy when we decided to make territorial wines instead of selling it unbottled, and when we put up our prices,' continues Boris, 'but then we'd discover that he was telling his friends in town how proud he was of us.'

The hardest moment always came when the green harvest required the cutting away of grape bunches. 'People of that generation believed in the 'more is more' credo,' says David. 'We had to convince him that there was another way, that reducing a vine's production from 10 kgs to 1.5 made sense.'

In that same year, Carlo had split the family farm with his brother, Luigi, where they had worked together under their surname, Buzzinelli. Their father, Gigi, had been among the first Collio estates to bottle its wines in the 1960s, along with Livio Felluga and Gradnik. 'Our *nonno* was someone who used his brains more than his brawn,' says David. 'He taught a lot of people here how to prune or graft both vines and fruit trees. It was our grandmother who kept the farm going.' The family's four cows were sold in the early '70s, and the peach and cherry trees gradually gave way to vines. 'You can't run a mixed farm and make wine well at the same time,' he says.

On his side, Carlo was lucky to have two sons as able and enthusiastic about wine. David is a tall, strapping young man who wears his hair long like a viking. The brothers work together on all aspects of the estate, but David is usually in charge of vinification; he's also on the Consortium's council. Boris handles the vineyards and the office work. Carlo is always on hand to proffer advice and the wisdom of his experience. Together they have built a large new functional cellar big enough to accommodate groups of up to 50 people for winetastings.

The estate totals fifteen hectares, of which seven are in the Collio and the rest in Isonzo. From the Collio, the Buzzinellis produce 35,000 bottles of which 10,000 are Pinot Grigio. Sauvignon is bottled separately, and is rich and aromatic, as is Friulano which is made both macerated and not. They also produce 2,000 bottles of Collio Bianco, a blend of Pinot Bianco with Tocai, Sauvignon and a little Malvasia. Since 2005 that wine spends some time in wood. The estate's red is a Merlot that ages for two years in wood.

The family's focus now is on extracting the minerality and character from Pradis' excellent terroir. 'We have a special microclimate here,' says David, 'as Pradis is the first hill up from the plain and feels the influence of the sea close by, which adds warmth and fullness to our wines.'

Malvasia Istriana

Wine

Picéch

Pradis, 11
Cormòns
TEL 0481 60347
www.picech.com

Roberto Picéch is one of the most respected of the new generation of Collio producers, not only for the personal stamp he has been able to give his wines, but also for the story of how he began to make them. His father, Egidio, was known as 'il Ribel', the rebel, and had a very forceful character. 'He did a lot for Friuli's wines, was strong and proud, and angry at the world,' says his son, Roberto, who is now in his forties and one of the Consortium's councillors. 'I often had to battle with him to win his approval for my winemaking. In some ways that slowed me down, but ultimately it may not have been such a bad thing.'

Roberto's grandfather had come to Pradis in the 1920s to work on the lands of Count Savorgnan as a tenant farmer under the *mezzadria* (sharecropping) system. In 1963, Egidio was able to buy five hectares of that land at auction when the feudal farm went bankrupt after the count's death. 'Like some of my friends' fathers, Egidio was brought up in poverty and found the idea of reducing yields to improve quality anathema.' Roberto had been on trips to France and had seen the positive effect of rigour in the vineyards. The two fought bitterly about it. 'My father would say: "I used to make two or three times the amount of wine you do, and I sold it easily; now you have less and can't sell it all." That was a constant argument between us,' says Roberto. 'He'd been to France too, but he couldn't see the potential of those changes.' Two years before his father's death, Roberto bought the winery from him. He dedicated his most

The 'Queen of the Vines' in the vineyards of Pradis

complex white to his mother, Jelka. 'I owe her a lot: she worked as we did, drove the tractor, and managed to keep us kept us all together,' says Roberto, who now lives at Pradis with his lovely wife Alessia, and their young daughter Athena. He has just completed work on a large new cellar under the house.

Picéch makes four whites – Malvasia Istriana, Friulano, Pinot Bianco, and Collio Bianco Jelka; and two reds, as well as a Passito di Pradis entirely from Malvasia grapes. Bianco di Jelka is a native blend of Ribolla, Tocai Friulano and Malvasia. Here the Malvasia is macerated for 30 hours and vinified separately from the other grapes, which are worked together. The other grapes are macerated on the skins for eight days before being matured in barriques of differing ages. The wine is assembled, unfiltered, in May. Of a soft burnished gold, this wine has a complex nose of stone-fruits that is underpinned by a more earthy palate and a long, lightly spiced finale. 'Thanks to Gravner, people are no longer afraid of unfiltered wines,' says Roberto. 'Not long ago, if you didn't have a consultant winemaker, a network of agents, technical equipment and French barriques, people thought you couldn't make wine. But instead, wine is made in the vineyards, and you can use an old-fashioned press to get just as good or better results than some supermodern equipment. What counts in the Collio is to make your own personality felt.'

Wine

Doro Princic

Pradis, 5
Cormòns
TEL 0481 60723
doroprincic@virgilio.it

'If you open a bottle of my wine, there will never be any left, it will all be drunk,' says Sandro Princic goodnaturedly, as he pours me a glass of his marvellous Tocai Friulano. Its nutty perfumes, clean entry and salty minerality keep it elegant and fresh – and keep you going back for more. So too do the other wines in Sandro Princic's stable, including one of the finest of all Pinot Biancos, a floral yet earthed Malvasia, and a remarkable Sauvignon; he even makes a lovely warm and drinkable Merlot. While we taste the wines, Sandro's wife, Grazia comes in with platefuls of prosciutto, cheese and other savoury snacks. 'We're always in the mood to eat here,' he laughs wryly. This must be the most hospitable couple in Italian wine.

Sandro Princic admits to a passion for his own Malvasia: 'I think I drink most of it myself!' This jovial, down to earth character who looks more like a wrestler than a wine connoisseur attains a finesse about his wines that is the envy of many. 'It all comes down to two things: a terroir like ours at Pradis, and great grapes that you try not to spoil in the cellar. Pradis is sunny and hot, yet the soil gives the minerality that stops the wines from becoming cloying,' he explains. Princic is an advocate of vinifying *'in bianco'* – without wood. 'No one wants wood any more on this kind of wine. I like steel or, even better, cement tanks for my whites,' he says. 'They still use cement in Bordeaux: it's a natural insulator. We get enough structure here without needing added weight or vanilla from barriques. I want to respect the Collio's soil, so I don't fertilize. All I do is reduce the quantity of grapes my vines produce.'

Sandro took over running the small ten-hectare estate from his father, Doro, who was a legendary figure in the Collio's history and who first settled in Pradis in 1939. 'In the early days this was a mixed farm of animals, vegetables and vines,' he says. 'My father always liked to say that the wine was better appreciated when it was in bottles, so he was one of the first to do it here. He lived to be 92 and was as much a part of the Pradis

Sandro Princic

*Pradis vineyards
after rain*

landscape as the vineyards he planted, always giving help and
advice to anyone who needed it.' It's a couple of weeks before
the harvest, and Sandro shakes his head as he tastes one of the
wines. 'When the grapes are maturing, the wine is never quite as
good: it's something to do with nature's energy.' Sandro's energy
is all dedicated to his house, his family – including his son Carlo
who helps make the wines – and his vineyards. You'll always
find him there, contented as long as he doesn't have to stray too
far from the gentle hills of Pradis.

Subida, Novali, Plessiva and Zegla

I've grouped all the wineries from this area together in alphabet-
ical order as they are geographically united, even if their
addresses differ. The extensive 33-hectare wood of Plessiva is a
nature reserve, and covers large areas of Monte Quarin. Its
chestnut, acacia, oak and other deciduous trees are a perfect
habitat for varied birds, flora and fauna. Its influence on the
vineyards below and around it is palpable: they receive much
cooler air in summer, which helps the aromatic grapes –
Sauvignon, and the Pinots Grigio and Bianco – to maintain their
perfumes. Higher on the hill, at Monte, the vineyards are surrounded by woods and, of course, by the wildlife that inhabits
them. Subida is the pass in the valley between Cormòns and the
vineyards of Plessiva and Zegla as the road curves towards
Slovenia. In the warm amphitheatre known as Zegla, the
harvest often comes a full ten days ahead of Oslavia (see chapter 1). This is another key cru for Tocai Friulano, which reveals
itself here well structured, warm and complex.

Subida

Subida
Cormòns
TEL OSTERIA
0481 61689
TEL TRATTORIA
0481 60531
www.lasubida.it
PRICE OSTERIA €€
PRICE TRATTORIA €€€€

Trattoria de la Subida

Sautéed guinea fowl

Restaurants, Agriturismo, Riding Stables
Trattoria al Cacciatore de la Subida

There just isn't enough space here to do justice to the remark-able contribution Josko Sirk and his family have made to the Collio's territory. Sirk is a tireless innovator. He runs two of the area's most successful restaurants (see below), an artisan vinegar factory, a lovely agriturismo with 16 houses set in tended gardens with a swimming pool, tennis courts and even a stable for riding. As if that were not enough, he has long been a champion of the Collio's wines, and has been involved in many of its promotional campaigns, including the recent yellow Vespas. He's friends with all the winemakers, has an intimate knowledge and appreciation of their wines – from the most classic to the most innovative – and has helped launch several estates though his loyal clientèle. One look at the restaurant's incredible wine list is proof of this commitment. I've been particularly impressed too by his ability to seek out small local food producers and arti-sans, and help publicize and keep them going.

Despite having been born in Subida, Sirk has never forgotten his Slovenian origins. At 'La Subida', as his great restaurant is known locally, you are just as likely to discover an exciting new wine from a young Slovenian winemaker as you are to sample a recent Collio discovery. If this was true when the barriers were still in place between the two countries – their political border was less than a mile from La Subida – it's even more so now. Indeed, Josko Sirk is actively working to bring the two sides of what is palpably the same terroir together.

As for the restaurants, there are two: Osteria de la Subida is located just down and across the road from the main restaurant, and offers a very relaxed place for a salad or plate of cheeses, pasta or thinly sliced carpaccio. In season you'll find the simple but delicious dishes locals eat in their homes, such as *frittata con le erbe*, an omelette flavoured with young herb leaves. There are wines by the glass or bottle to accompany the dishes. In summer the outdoor tables on the two terraces are always full of winemakers, cyclists, walkers and other Collio visitors, taking in the sunshine over an informal meal.

The main restaurant is quite unique, in my experience. To me it feels like going to eat in a private country house, with the whole family there in attendance. Josko Sirk's wife, Loredana, is always elegant in her long dresses that speak of another time; her daughter, Erika, helps in the dining room, as does the radiant Tanja, who also has one foot in the kitchen: her new

Josko and Loredana Sirk in the restaurant

husband, Alessandro Gavagna, is La Subida's talented chef. Mitja, the Sirk's son, is also present when he's not studying. At the heart of the restaurant is a fireplace, open to all sides. Its warmth offers the wooden-beamed rooms their focal point and the traditional place to cook the polenta that accompanies so many of the restaurant's dishes. The Sirks have come up with an ingenious machine that slowly stirs the golden cornflour as it cooks. The menu alternates between light, creative use of native ingredients and the hearty country recipes that characterize this part of north-eastern Italy. Bitter radicchio leaves are sweetened with slices of apple and horseradish *(kren)*, then topped with melted cheese. Pastas are hand-made of farro and served with wild mushrooms; potato gnocchi come filled with plums and sprinkled with cinnamon. Sirk is a keen hunter, and the restaurant's official name, Trattoria al Cacciatore, signals the presence of both hunters and their catch: in season you'll find hare and boar as well as any number of game birds on the menu. One of the keystones of La Subida's repertoire is *stinco di vitello*, or roasted veal shanks: they come almost caramelized from their slow cooking, and are served with potatoes roasted in an earthenware *teccia*. If you're unsure which wines best suit these dishes, let the excellent sommelier, Michele Paiano, guide you. He seems part of the family too, and shares their energy and enthusiasm. Save room for desserts, the Slovenian pastries are a fine ending to this inspiring, cross-cultural meal.

OTHER AGRITURISMI

Al Confine (Plessiva, 3; tel 0481-630451, 338-1955948; www.al-confine.it) Aldo Russian's Bed & Breakfast is surrounded by woods and vineyards in a peaceful part of one of the Collio's greatest winemaking zones. The family offers three double rooms and one apartment.

Al Poc Da Subid – Marisa Cucit (Monte,10, Cormòns; tel 0481 61004; www.alpocdasubide.com) In a rustic 18th-century stone house with wooden balconies, this B&B offers five rooms in a panoramic position.

Borgo San Daniele (Via San Daniele, 16, Cormòns; tel 0481 60552; www.borgosandaniele.it) Mauro and Alessandra Mauri have created one of the most beautiful places to stay in the area: three element-themed rooms with all the sophisti-cated detailing you'd expect from these great winemakers.

Casa Mafalda – Andrea Losetti (Pradis, 23; tel 0481 630601, 328 3255170; casa.mafalda@virgilio.it) This B&B is situated in a converted barn at Pradis, in the heart of the winemaking area. It offers five rooms.

Casa del Riccio (Monte, 1; tel 338 6229674; www.casadelriccio.it) Commanding wonderful views of Monte Quarin and the vineyards of the Cormòns Collio, this estate produces its own wines. As B&B it offers its guests four rooms in lovely farm buildings that have been converted very comfortably.

Casa Riz (Giassico, 18, Cormòns; tel 0481 61362; www.casariz.com) Alessandro Riz's winery and agriturismo are situated in an unspoiled borgo near Cormòns. At weekends you can sample some of the area's local foods with wines in the trattoria, or stay overnight in one of its pretty, modest rooms.

Il Gallo Rosso (Pradis, 20; tel 0481 60902; www.buzzinelli.com) Maurizio Buzzinelli's family has long been a mainstay of Pradis. Here they offer four bedrooms for B&B, accompanied by their fine estate-made wines.

Tana dei Ghiri (Monte, 40; tel 0481 61951; www.tanadeighiri.gooditaly.net) This attractive agriturismo offers the most spectacular views from high up on Monte Quarin, overlooking the town of Cormòns; on a clear day you can see the sea.

Tonut (Via Isonzo, 2/bis, Cormòns; tel 0481-61440) Gianni Tonut sells his own wines accompanied by simple country snacks: rustic soups, *salumi*, frittatas, cheeses. Closed Tuesday and Wednesday; open all year.

Opposite: Artisan-made cheeses at La Subida

Wine

Zegla, 20
Cormòns
TEL 0481 639826
No email

Branko

The Branko cellar and house are across the road from the local school, at the valley junction between the hills of Novali and Zegla. Igor Erzetic, Branko's son, has taken over running this small family estate, some of whose six hectares of vineyards are situated within what is known as the Zegla cru – a particularly favourable terroir for Tocai Friulano; Branko is also well known for a fine Pinot Grigio. Igor has given the cellar and wines a modernist touch: spare lines, clean wines.

'When I finished my studies in œnology at Cividale, I wanted to join my father in making our wines, but we only had three hectares then and there just wasn't enough work for both of us,' says Igor Erzetic. He spent a few years helping his father part-time as he gained experience in other, bigger wineries in Friuli.

Igor Erzetic and his dog

'In 2000, when my father was in his mid seventies, I came back full time,' Igor says. 'That's when the generational divide took place.' If Branko had been brought up to believe that the vines should be encouraged to produce as much as possible, Igor's peers were already proving that reducing yields led to much higher quality. 'The first thing to do was to cut them back, as well as to increase the number of vines per hectare from 2,000 to 5,500 whenever we replanted. I think it's been hard for my father, who is a tough nut, to accept the idea of dis-carding healthy bunches of grapes before they reach maturity – it goes against everything his spent his life doing. Indeed, when it's time for that kind of pruning, he stays indoors.' The vines now produce around 1.5 kilos of grapes each. In the flatter vineyards beside the cellar, it's Sauvignon and Pinot Grigio that do best, as they prefer moister terrains. Up on the Zegla hillside, where there is more *ponca* and the soils are poorer and warmer, Tocai and Chardonnay ripen more succesfully. Between these four single-variety whites and a red, a blend of Merlot with a little Cabernet Sauvignon, the output is a total of 45,000 bottles.

The grapes are brought into the cellar very quickly after harvesting, within one hour whenever possible. The must is brought down to 19°C in a serpentine cooler, then passed into steel tanks to decant for 15 hours before being pumped into the fermentation vats with selected yeasts. The whites are worked with just a little wood, the main bulk of the wines being kept in stainless steel. 'I don't use barriques for them, but larger 400-litre barrels of French oak,' he explains. 'My Sauvignon is the exception, as it is made entirely in steel to maintain its fruit qualities.' So what does the wood add to the other wines? 'In

2007, just 5% of our Tocai Friulano and 25% of the Chardonnay were fermented in the barrel, and left on the lees until January, when they were added to the steel-only batches. Doing this seems to give the wines a bit more complexity.' Igor takes all the winemaking decisions himself: 'That way I can honestly say they reflect my tastes.'

Does he make a Collio Bianco blend? 'No. I feel that the Collio blend lacks personality, that you're never quite sure what you're drinking. I prefer wines with a recognizable identity card.'

And the future? 'Each time you finish the harvest, despite having given it your all, you realize there's room for improvement. That's what gives you the impetus to go ahead and try even harder the following year.'

Wine

Zegla, 1bis
Cormòns
TEL 0481 60798
www.gasparebuscemi.com

Gaspare Buscemi

Gaspare Buscemi is a self-styled *enologo vinificatore artigiano*, or artisan winemaker and consultant œnologist. Why the word artisan? 'In Italy, all the best products stem from an artisanal base,' he says, as we talk at his vinification cellar. 'The artisan has a natural talent to transform his raw materials manually, to the best of his creative abilities. If industry looks to the global demands of the wine market and its trends, the artisan is more likely to be driven by personal, experimental and cultural motives. In France these *vignerons* are respected for being individualists yet they have known how to organize themselves in groups. We haven't been as successful with that type of approach in Italy: I'd like to unite the little producers in Italy in a similar way, to strengthen our positions.'

Buscemi, whose father was Sicilian and mother Slovenian, was born in Valdobbiadene and began work there in a wine co-operative. In the early 1960s, he did a stint for Marco Felluga and later became the technical adviser of the Collio's Consortium before setting up his own service centre for helping small wine producers. 'I was active on lots of fronts, working with what are now the fathers and grandfathers of today's Collio wine-makers.' As the demands for fine wines grew in the 1970s, Buscemi used his palate and experience to select and blend small batches of the *contadini*'s wines into exclusive products. 'I really believed in their potential, and put their individual names on the labels, gaining praise from critics like Veronelli,' he explains.

In 1976 he moved to his current house and cellar in the valley below Zegla. By then he had large contracts with distributors and would assemble wines to meet their demands. 'At that time, it offered the *contadini* the possibility to work their vines peacefully during the year, knowing they had a market for their wines. I helped them with any technical problems in the vineyards and cellars. The trouble was that the markets were clamouring for only Pinot Grigio – 90% of our sales were for that. Indeed, we could never keep up with demand as most of the growers had more than ten or twenties varieties in their vineyards.'

It all became too much. In the Isonzo plain, Pinot Grigio was being produced to the maximum of the vines' capabilities, sacrificing quality for quantity, so Buscemi shut down that business and dedicated himself to other aspects of winemaking. He travelled throughout Italy, and still works in Tuscany, Lazio and Piedmont, operating as a technical consultant to many family run wineries. He owns no vineyards, but produces wines from grapes he selects and buys.

I was fascinated to discover that Buscemi is also an inventor of machines related to vinification. His large warehouse is home to a whole cast of prototypes and original designs that resemble Willy Wonka's: hand-made presses to be used in the vineyard to reduce the risk of must-oxidization to a minimum; spiral tube-drying stands; machines to wash and purify corks so as to minimize the risk of phenol contamination; large nets to hold the cap down in the barrel...the imaginative list is endless.

As an experimentor, Buscemi has made wines without recourse to correctors, extracting the most from the grapes without the tricks and shortcuts often favoured by industry. He produces a line of *spumanti sur lie*, using the grapes' natural sugars, with a cuvée called Perle d'Uva, whose vintages from the late 1980s are still deliciously drinkable.

Gaspare Buscemi's key hobby horse is for long-ageing wines. His cellars contain bottles from over twenty vintages, and his wines, be they sparkling or still, offer the interested taster the proof that the Collio is eminently capable of producing old and very old wines – both white and red – of excellent minerality and structure. Buscemi often holds vertical tastings to prove it. 'What matters is to sell *vino*: our wine, its culture and its territory,' he says. His is surely the culture of diversity, patently rolled into one man.

Wine

Colle Duga

Zegla, 10
Cormòns
TEL 0481 61177
www.colleduga.com

Damian Princic's estate, Colle Duga, is perched on the slopes of the Zegla hills, right on the border with Slovenia. Indeed, until the frontier fell in December 2007, armed guards used to patrol his vineyards to make sure no one slipped through. 'We got used to it and, in a certain way, felt safer then as you certainly didn't

Zegla with Colle Duga

need keys with those guys around,' says Damian, wrily. 'But of course we're much happier now.' Damian has nine hectares of vineyards scattered within a three-kilometre range of the family's house and cellar, including up by Russiz and La Subida. That's not unusual as the plots in this part of the Collio tend to be very small, often less than one hectare each. 'If you are born a *contadino*, it's very hard to exchange or sell a piece of land that has always been in the family, or was bought by your grandfather. They're as much a part of you as your house.' Damian should know, as the small estate was bought, parcel by parcel, by his grandfather and father over many years. Damian was 21 when he took over from his father, in 1991. Up until then the family had sold what wine they made *sfuso*, or un-bottled, to wholesalers who came to drain the cellars in this area for wine to resell in the towns. Damian had worked with the family from childhood, but after his military service he came back to run the winery and start making changes to improve the quality. He became interested in many aspects of wine culture in the Collio, and is a member of the Consortium's council.

As we walk through the vineyards, Damian explains the transitions in planting styles the Collio has seen (for more detail, see p. 26). 'In the old vineyards, before tractors, the people here used draught cattle. Now we have other ways to lessen the soil's compacting, by planting grass between the rows or in alternate rows and, with wide tyres on our tractors, we don't do much damage. We're returning to the idea of using natural fertilizers too, such as manure. But realistically, we can't go back to the horse, no matter how poetic it seems. There are good ways of using modern machinery that is light and non-compacting.'

Damian's generation have learned from the mistakes of their older relatives. 'If, in the 1970s, they all planted what the market seemed to want – and that went in waves according to fashion – now we plant what works best for a specific site.' Damian began bottling in 1998. He works closely with his father, wife and children. If there have been generational tensions about how to work the vines, they have largely been resolved, and even his father now joins in the *diradamento*, or 'green pruning' of the excess bunches. Sometimes, his father pushes to harvest earlier than Damian wants; Damian resists. 'Nature makes you take very fast decisions at times, and you have to follow your instincts,' he says. 'We used only to trust a result if it came out of a lab, but now I am much more likely to harvest after tasting the grapes. I prefer wines that reflect the flavours and perfumes of the grapes on the vine.'

That's why he vinifies some varieties purely in steel, to retain as much as possible of this natural character; others do their fermentation and ageing in wood. Damian's wines are characterized by fine minerality, balance and an unmistakable link to their terroir. The Collio Bianco is intriguing and complex, a blend of Tocai, Sauvignon, Malvasia Istriana and Chardonnay. 'This is the hardest wine to sell,' he says, 'but it's worth making because it is bigger than the sum of its parts.'

Princic sometimes asks for help from the outside. 'It can be very useful to have someone come in with a fresh palate to help in the tasting.' Giorgio Bertossi, a producer from Palmanova, plays that role for Damian before the Colle Duga wines are bottled each year. The wines are also known for being good value for money.

The Princic's wines have won many awards, especially for the Tocai – soon to be called simply 'Friulano'. 'I still feel annoyed that the name Tocai was just thrown away: we should have fought harder to keep it.'

Wine, Jazz Club, Wine Bar
Gradnik

Plessiva, 5
Cormòns
TEL 0481 61395
www.gradnik.it

Neda Gradnik comes out to greet me from under the most magnificent oak tree. It's vast and fills the whole courtyard in front of her villa, which sits at the top of the vine-covered valley at Plessiva. From her walled terrace, behind the house, you can see past the undulating Zegla vineyards, all the way to the Slovenian mountains behind Gorizia in one direction, and to the Dolomites in the other. Inside, the large house is filled with modern paintings. Underneath it is a warren of sloping tunnels which lead into the vaulted cellar she's turned into a successful jazz club and

Gradnik villa seen from Edi Keber's vineyards

meeting place. For a very modest price you can join her *'circolo'* and partake of the music and wine combo she offers.

'My parents had a bar in Cormòns when I was growing up,' she explains, 'and I love being around lots of people.' Neda's father was Gradimiro, or Miro, Gradnik, one of the Collio's pioneer winemakers and early bottlers. He began the estate in 1957, building it up over the years to 200 hectares. Luigi Veronelli and Mario Soldati, two of Italy's most important wine writers – and pioneers in their own right – wrote with affection and admiration about Gradnik and his wines. Soldati, in a wonderful book about his gastronomic travels in 1970, *Vino al Vino*, describes Miro Gradnik as a one-man-band when it came to his wines, working tirelessly as vine-pruner, winemaker, businessman and labourer. And the result? Wines that Soldati put on the same pedestal as the Barolos and Barbarescos of Piemonte. Wines of Pinot Grigio that were 'gold with pinkish highlights or, rather, the colour of pale bricks'. Gradnik explained that their character was due to the land having been left uncultivated for decades after the ravages of the First World War, and only replanted in the 1930s and 40s, so the soil was 'new, very rich in all its salts and natural mineral substances'. Soldati was amazed that, in 1970, Gradnik had no telephone. Thinking about it though, he decided that only a man so confident of the superior quality of his wines and of the loyalty of its drinkers could afford to live without such a fundamental means of communication

Neda now runs one-third of her father's estate. With the help of her three children, Mirta, Melita and Miro, and her mother, Romana, she keeps this multi-cultural winery going. Miro is studying œnology, and helps her do the work in the vineyards. Melita assists with the tastings and day to day running of the business. Igor Branca, a technical consultant, also lends a hand. Neda herself drives the tractor and determines that there shall be no weedkillers in the vineyards, and as little spraying as possible on the grapes. A real *Donna del Vino*, or woman of wine.

As we sit in the shade on a hot summer's day, Neda presents me with a glass of wine of a surprisingly yellow colour. 'Guess what this is,' she says, mischievously. I can't identify it, but I know one thing: it's a very young, very old wine. It turns out to be a Traminer from 1989, whose natural acidity and tension between sweet and dry has kept it alive for all this time. 'That's the Plessiva vineyard for you!' she exclaims proudly.

Wine, Agriturismo

Edi Keber

Zegla, 17
Cormòns
TEL 0481 61184
edikeber@tin.it
www.agriturismofvg.com

Edi Keber is one of the most dynamic wine producers in the Collio. He's been an active ambassador not only of its native grapes but also of the territory itself, and continues to contribute energy and ideas to the promotion of this unique viticultural area. He is on the council of the Consortium, and has promoted the Collio's recent yellow Vespa initiative. His lovely house and cellar sit up on the hilltop of Zegla, commanding views of the Plessiva vineyards and forest and also of the Slovenian hills as they lead into the Giulian Alps. Edi and his son, Kristian, work the land that was once cultivated by his father and grandfather. Edi's mother, Metoda, still hoes her vegetable patch and cares for the vineyards as if they were an extension of her garden. Edi's wife, Silvana, and young daughter, Veronika, run a beautiful agriturismo with several rooms above the cellar. It's laid out on different sides of a courtyard that is always full of visitors and friends dropping by to see Edi or taste a glass of his very characterful wines. They reflect Edi's strength. 'Around here, I'm in charge,' he likes to say. *'A casa mia, comando io!'*

Edi Keber and his son, Kristian

In his winemaking, too, Edi has very clear ideas, including about vinification tanks. 'Cement gives better results,' he says. 'I understood that wood was better but steel was not, so I've excluded it. Steel has no soul.' For someone in a white-wine producing area, this means taking a stand. In recent years he's also taken a stand by deciding to make only one white wine, instead of the portfolio of single-varietal wines many of his

Metoda Keber working in her vegetable garden

peers make. 'I wanted to focus on the white blend that most expresses the complexity of our area, a wine I call simply "Collio",' he says. 'Eliminating the word 'Bianco' from its title will push people to make a bigger effort to understand what the Collio is all about,' he says. The blend is of 70% Tocai Friulano, 10% Malvasia Istriana, 10% Ribolla Gialla and 10% of Pinots Grigio and Bianco. He has also introduced an unfiltered version of the same wine. The Kebers also produce one red wine, a Collio Rosso of Merlot and Cabernet Franc. Current production from the estate's twelve hectares of vineyards is of about 60,000 bottles of the white, and 7,000 red. 'In 1985 there were only four producers making Collio Bianco, but in 1996 the disciplinare changed to give us more flexibility.' Why the unfiltered version? 'Because too much of a wine's goodness is lost in the filtering,' he says.

'In the '80s I ripped out most of my Pinot Grigio, Sauvignon and Chardonnay and everyone thought I was crazy,' he says. 'To take out what people wanted and put in what they didn't (Tocai), was to go against the flow, *contro corrente*, but I remembered that my father and grandfather's Tocais were always great, and it's very constant here at Zegla. Tocai is naturally generous and you need to contain it, but this is its best terroir: our *flysh* gives it character and minerality.'

There are of course some rules to making quality wines from the Tocai Friulano, even here: Edi aims for 1.5 kg of grapes per plant, 50-60 quintals of grapes per hectare. 'Pick the grapes when they are almost over-mature, starting to turn brownish, and they'll give an Alsatian, mineral quality you can't get when they are still green. You have just ten days to pick it when it's like this, or they'll rot and drop. And it's not true that you lose acidity waiting this long: my wines last ten years easily.' Once in the cellar, Edi Keber leaves his wines on the yeasts for six months, to increase flavour and personality. Indeed, they have loads of it, just like their maker.

Wine, Agriturismo

WINERY:
Zegla, 15
Cormòns
TEL 0481 639844
AGRITURISMO:
Zegla, 19 bis
Cormòns
TEL 0481 226899
www.renatokeber.com

Renato Keber

The gently curving hillside called Zegla, close by the border with Slovenia, has long been home to Renato Keber and his family. Renato's great grandfather, Franc, came from nearby Vipulzano to settle here in 1900, when this was still under Austrian rule. 'They were farmers producing fruit, grapes and hay for the Austrian army,' explains Renato as we look east towards the contours of the higher Slovenian hills. 'They made a little wine from their terraced vineyards and sold it by the barrel to the Hapsburg court at Vienna,' he says. 'Most of it was Ribolla, which they called Rebùla. My grandmother came from Visnjevik, a high Brda hilltown known for its Ribolla.' Renato's father, Miroslavo, and his siblings were born at Zegla, as was Renato. Today, the older generation still help out in the vine-yards, which are cared for entirely by the extended family. (Renato and Edi's fathers were first cousins; the two estates are next to each other but run separately). 'My father and uncle created all these terraces by hand, breaking through the rock and planting the vines without tractors,' he says.

There was only one bicycle in the family when Renato was courting. He was lucky: his lovely wife, Savina, lived just across the border in Slovenia, at Medana. Today it's a few minutes' walk from one house to the other; in those days the border line was guarded with dogs, rifles and a curfew which made for a lot of cycling when the border gate was closed. Savina runs the couples' attractive agriturismo, helped at times by their young daughter, Tereza (see below).

Savina and Tereza Keber

'In the 1950s we sold to wine merchants who would set their prices here,' says Renato. 'It went to innkeepers and osterie.' In 1976, the year of the two Friuli earthquakes, the Kebers' cellar was enlarged and a new house built. 'In 1977 my father first used the new cellar, using a newly bought second-hand press,' Renato recalls. 'What an improvement!' Renato learned more about winemaking by studying and working for some of the top Collio estates. 'In 1987, we began to bottle our wines and lower the yields in the vineyards,' he says. In the early 1990s Renato met the great importer Marc De Grazia, and became one of the first small Collio producers to export to the USA. 'I realized that only by harvesting very ripe grapes could I express the

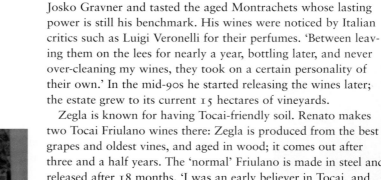

*Zegla with Monte
Quarin and Plessiva
behind*

Renato Keber

character of our terroir,' he says. 'I never wanted my wines to be paper white or made using much technology, so I gave them a little skin contact in the vinification.' He visited France with Josko Gravner and tasted the aged Montrachets whose lasting power is still his benchmark. His wines were noticed by Italian critics such as Luigi Veronelli for their perfumes. 'Between leaving them on the lees for nearly a year, bottling later, and never over-cleaning my wines, they took on a certain personality of their own.' In the mid-90s he started releasing the wines later; the estate grew to its current 15 hectares of vineyards.

Zegla is known for having Tocai-friendly soil. Renato makes two Tocai Friulano wines there: Zegla is produced from the best grapes and oldest vines, and aged in wood; it comes out after three and a half years. The 'normal' Friulano is made in steel and released after 18 months. 'I was an early believer in Tocai, and began working it in wood in 1988. It's a difficult grape as it can over-ripen and drop from the vine, yet it must be as mature as possible.' In addition to wines of Pinot Grigio, Chardonnay, Pinot Bianco and three Sauvignons – including the Grici Sauvignon, which is released after four and a half years – Keber also make a wine from Ribolla Gialla called Extreme. 'Here the grapes are macerated for one month in open cement tanks using wild yeasts without temperature controls,' he says. It is aged in large barrels without racking, and released after two and a half years, as is Beli Grici, the Collio white blend of Pinot Bianco, Ribolla and other white grapes. Keber also makes two reds. 'I've always been drawn to secondary and tertiary perfumes, so I aim for wines that are expressive and have enough vitality to keep them young as they age. The Collio terroir's minerality helps me achieve these goals.'

You can't miss Zegla's red house: it stands out for miles in the sea of vines that surround it. Here Savina and Renato Keber have created one of the Collio's most appealing agriturismi, opened in 2008. The conversion of the large house into four apartments and two rooms was entirely done by Savina with Liviana Fedel, and their very personal touch is apparent in every detail of the simply elegant interiors, where hand-woven natural fabrics are used with country antiques to great effect. There are kitchens in some of the apartments, and a garden to enjoy the home-baked breakfasts, as well as wi-fi connections for those of us who can never switch off.

Wine

Plessiva, 13
Cormòns
TEL 0481 61027
aldopolencic@virgilio.it

Aldo and Ferdinando Polencic

Aldo Polencic is a soft-spoken, opinionated, forty-something winemaker. His output of just 20,000 bottles is one of the smallest in the Collio – or in Friuli for that matter – a choice that Polencic maintains with determination. 'The only way to make the kind of wine I have in mind is to drastically reduce the yields and insist on stringent selection when you bring the grapes into the cellar,' he says. He owns six hectares of vine-yards, rents one other and buys in some grapes from older Tocai vineyards; his production per hectare is of around 30 quintals. All of Polencic's wines go into wood. His newly constructed ageing cellar has separate rooms for the white and red wines being aged in tonneaux and barriques.

'I'm not into too much technology,' he says. 'I prefer to use a 30-year-old roller-press that was my father's and that squeezes the must out slowly.' After decantation the white musts go into tonneaux to ferment and remain on the lees until June, with bâtonnages as necessary but no racking. Then they are bottled. They come out one year after the harvest. The reds follow what was once a traditional path: they are fermented in open-topped conical barrels before being pressed. A week-long natural decantation in steel vats follows before the must is pumped into smaller barrels, where it will stay for about two years, with fre-quent racking.

This use of wood necessarily brings added richness and struc-ture to Polencic's wines, as well as herbal notes from the wood and the minerality and verve that comes from having some of his key vineyards in the Plessiva area. 'I don't want to make banal wines: that may mean I have to charge more for them but

Aldo and Marinka Polencic

all the manual work that goes into making wines like this is costly,' he says as we visit a small rented vineyard below La Subida from which he makes his Merlot Unico. 'In 2006 I made just three barriques of wine from this plot, a few hundred bottles.' Other wines include Tocai Ulivi, Pinot Bianco Ulivi, Pinot Grigio DOC Collio; Merlot Ulivi and Tocai Unico, which is only produced in magnums.

The Polencic family has been traced back in this area for 400 years. One of Aldo's sisters, Marinka, is a free-lance œnologist who comes home often from Tuscany to taste with her brother and give him a hand – so the future of this generation's wines is in four good hands.

Aldo's father, Ferdinando, sold his wine unbottled before he became one of the Collio's first producers to bottle under his own name, in 1974. Ferdinando is a wonderful character. I met him during the harvest, with a large straw hat on his head he directed the pickers, signalling for the tractor to come and pick up the baskets of grapes as they were filled. 'The Collio has always been respected for its quality,' he says, as he clips bunches of Pinot Grigio. 'Indeed the Austrians used these wines in their church services. We've been here for four generations, with the old people contributing their wisdom long after their physical strength had faded. In the 1950s, I cried when many of my neighbours and friends left their farms to go and join the chair-making industry. At that time, they earned more in one month than I did in one year. Times were hard but I always felt they would swing around again, and now they have.' By then it was noon, and time for a jolly harvest lunch in the cool shade of the courtyard which I was very happy to join.

Harvest lunch at the Polencic cellar

Wine, Agriturismo
Isidoro Polencic

Plessiva, 12
Cormòns
TEL 0481 60655
www.polencic.com

When I last visited her, it was lunchtime, but Elisabetta Polencic was hard at work in her office, a room that has been carved out of the estate's large modern cellar building on the short hill that leads up from Novali to Plessiva. It's surrounded by woods and vineyards. The young woman was, as ever, charming and open.

'For us, home, work and the cellars are all one and the same,' she said. Elisabetta handles PR and visits to the winery, as well as overseeing the day to day management. Her brother, Michele, is the estate's winemaker and their younger brother, Alex, is finishing his degree in enology and will join the firm too. 'You'd think that we had been pushed into working here, but our parents never forced it on us; rather, they let us choose our own road, but urged us to stick to whatever job we selected.'

Isidoro, who died in 2008, gave Michele a lot of freedom when he handed over the reins of this substantial estate, with 26 hectares of vineyards, three-quarters of which are in the Collio, and the rest in Isonzo. The Collio vineyards are divided between those that surround the cellars, at Plessiva, and those on Monte Quarin and at Ruttars. 'Our family has been here at Plessiva since before my great-grandparents' time,' she says.

The large wood of Plessiva – now a protected park within the Cormòns *comune*, and a lovely destination for hiking or mountain biking – keeps the temperatures in the vineyards that surround it cooler, which helps maintain perfumes and freshness in whites such as Sauvignon and Pinot Bianco.

'My family's aim has always been to make wines that reflect the character of each single variety of grape, as they grow in our soils,' she says. 'So even when we use wooden barrels to allow certain wines to do the malolactic fermentation, they never dominate the fruit of the wines.'

A recent project for the Polencics has been to create a new wine, called Fisc, starting from three 90-year-old Tocai Friulano vines they found in a vineyard behind Cormòns on Monte Quarin. 'A new vineyard was created using these three mother plants, and the result is a classic Tocai as it used to be made, but of course with the help of modern winemaking experience,' she says. 'I love the grapes in this vineyard, as they are quite different from our other Tocais: these have medium-sized bunches of golden, well-spaced berries as opposed to the greener, compact bunches from other sites.' Fisc is fermented in large barrels and left on the lees for several months. It is bottled in April and sold in October. The wine was created by Isidoro with his children.

'Our father's legacy will continue to live here, as so much of

Elisabetta Polencic

Winter vineyards at Plessiva

our experience and knowledge about our territory and its wines were handed down to us by him as we were growing up, and that's something we'll cherish for ever,' she adds.

Elisabetta also runs a lovely small agriturismo in a pretty house across the street from the cellars, with views overlooking the vineyards of Zegla and the hills of Slovenia. The mini apartments have kitchens, so visitors can feel as if they too live in the midst of this beautiful landscape.

Wine

Ronco dei Tassi

Monte, 38
Cormòns
TEL 0481 60155
www.roncodeitassi.it

Fabio Coser's estate is at Montona, high on the northern-eastern slopes of Monte Quarin, facing the Slovenian mountains, and it's named for the badgers *(tassi)* that live in the woods surrounding it. 'We like to think of them as our thermometers: when the grapes are sweet enough for the picking, badger families come down at night to feast on them, standing on their hind legs. It's a sign too of how wild and unspoiled this habitat is.' Coser, who is from the Veneto, has always been actively involved in high-level winemaking in Friuli, at important wineries like Angoris and Ca'Ronesca, as well as making wines for Colmello di Grotta (see p. 221). He has long been a committed member of the Consortium, and has been on its council. In

Fabio Coser

1989 he was able finally to start his own family estate. He and his wife, Daniela, found a 10-hectare property with 3.5 hectares of vines and a large *casa colonica*, or tenant farmhouse, at its centre. 'It needed complete overhauling, but we decided to retain as much as possible of its rustic detailing,' he says. Since then the property has grown to its current 13 hectares of vineyards, with eight more being rented throughout the *comune* of Cormòns – including some of the area's oldest vineyards.

'I've always been drawn to vineyards of character,' Coser explains as we visit a spectacular site high above Cormòns, where very old Tocai Friulano vines live harmoniously with fruit trees and vegetable patches. Coser avoids using weedkillers, in respect of both the plants and the soil. 'To me, making wine is 70 percent about the territory and the vines, and 30 percent the work we do in the cellars.' He seeks out vineyards in high positions to maintain elegance and richness in his wines, at 200 metres on Mt. Quarin and above the Madonnina at Pradis. Once the grapes arrive in the cellar, modern technology is useful for protecting their character.

Coser believes that the Collio's strength lies in the diversity of the approaches to the making of its white wines, especially the Collio Bianco blend. 'It's great that we have room for personal interpretation and expression,' he says. 'After all, the Collio's 'classic' style is very recent and stems directly from the pioneering work of Mario Schiopetto in the 1970s. That's when our wines began to find their definition. We all have a a lot to thank him for.'

The Cosers makes their wines with the help of their two sons, Matteo and Enrico. Coser produces one red, a Bordeaux blend of Cabernets and Merlot, in homage to the French wines he so admires, but it is the whites which distinguish the Collio. Ronco dei Tassi's iconic Fosarin is made from a single vineyard whose vines are up to 70 years old. It is planted to the three indigenous varieties – Tocai, Ribolla Gialla, and Malvasia – with some Pinot Bianco. Fosarin 2004 was nominated best Italian white wine by the Slow Food Gambero Rosso guide. It's worked entirely in barriques of varying ages, but maintains its floral elegance and minerality. 'The Collio may be best known for its monovarietal wines but happily there are exceptions.'

Wine

Ronco di Zegla

Zegla, 12
Cormòns
TEL 0481 61155
mauriziozegla@libero.it

Before the Second World War, Maurizio Princic's grandfather, Giuseppe, grew vegetables – *zucchine*, beans and cucumbers – and cherries for selling at the markets of Trieste and Cormòns.

'They also kept a few cows in the barn for their milk,' says Maurizio, who now runs the estate on the sloping hills of Zegla with his mother, Fides, and father, also called Giuseppe. 'When he died, in 1990, there were just two and a half hectares of vineyards, but in 1992 my parents and I decided to change policies here and dedicate our energies to vine-growing.' Today the estate totals 22 hectares of land, of which eight are planted to vines, with thirteen given over to cereal crops in the valley. Maurizio lives with his wife, Ambra, and their young daughter, Giada.

'In the '90s, my father sold wine in large tanks to brokers specializing in bulk wine, indeed, the whole of our cellar would be emptied in one swoop,' Maurizio continues. 'I was more interested in selling our wine in smaller quantities, establishing a direct rapport with the bars and restaurants, so we first brought in *damigiane*, the large basket-covered bottles holding 28 or 54 litres, and then bottles.' In 1997, the first year of bottling, 7,000 bottles were produced as well as the traditional *damigiane*. Maurizio studied farming at Gradisca and later specialized in winemaking. 'With my generation there's been a big switch in the approach to working the land,' he says. 'My father and grandfather did everything manually, including digging the vineyards, but today we have another take on it, and want to make better wines, and luckily we have machinery that can help us with that in the countryside.'

Tractors and other machinery are blessed on the third Sunday of November. 'Each town around here takes it in turns to host this *festa*, with their parades of tractors and harvesters.'

For the last ten years, Maurizio has planted grass under the vines to stabilize the terrain and add humus to the soil. In winter, he uses a special tractor attachment to open up the compacted earth between the rows and allow more oxygen into the soil.

Princic is most interested in making wines with Sauvignon, Tocai Friulano and Ribolla Gialla, though he does have some Pinot Grigio and Chardonnay, as well as Cabernets that go into his only red wine, Rosso di Ronco di Zegla. For the whites, the Tocai, Pinot Grigio and Sauvignon are all worked in stainless steel, remaining on the 'noble' lees for ten months. Some of his Chardonnay is moved into new tonneaux after fermentation, while the Ribolla is all worked in tonneaux.

Wine

Zegla, 1
Cormòns
TEL 0481 60720
www.sturm.it

Sturm

Oscar Sturm's family settled at Zegla in the 1850s from Andritz, a district of Graz. 'When I was growing up, in the 1950s and '60s, ours was like so many small farms here, with a few animals, vegetable fields and some vines mixed in amongst the fruit trees,' says Sturm. 'In the 1970s we switched to just growing vines, but initially we sold the wine *sfuso*, unbottled.' If the first customers were locals, Oscar soon looked for international buyers. 'We used to plant our vineyards following the requests of the markets, which were then always looking for international varieties such as Sauvignon and Pinot Grigio, and they sold well,' he explains. 'Now when we plant we try to be more attentive to the character of the site we have, and to plant vines that will do well in them, such as Tocai Friulano.'

View from Russiz towards Zegla and Slovenia

Sturm, who has two sons and a daughter, has ten hectares divided into one- and two-hectare parcels in and around Zegla. One larger vineyard is above the plain at Russiz, and was planted in the 1970s. 'In those days, we were allowed to do big earthworks to create flat vineyards that were easier to work,' he says. 'But that system was found to disrupt the underlying structure of the land too much, and today is no longer possible.' The new vineyards are trained to Guyot, with grass between the rows to help the vines maintain their equilibrium.

With his sons Patrick, a winemaker, and Denis, Oscar Sturm now produces a line of ten wines: six whites and four reds for a total of around 70,000 bottles. This includes a Collio Bianco blend of Pinot Grigio and Sauvignon named for their native town of Andritz, as well as a red Collio blend of Merlot and Cabernet Sauvignon.

'I feel that the white Collio blend is a positive wine for our area, as it gives each producer freedom to choose which grapes to use, but I'd never want to give up the single-variety wines. Too many people appreciate their separate identities,' he says. Most of the Sturm whites are made entirely in steel, though the Collio Bianco is worked in part in barriques, old and new. 'I prefer not to make my wines too heavy as they are made to go with our *cucina italiana*, which is generally a light cuisine.'

Wine

Novali, 12
Cormòns
TEL 0481 61327
www.vinitoros.com

Toros

Franco Toros is the quintessential Friulian host. At his family's estate at Novali, in the *comune* of Cormòns, everyone who stops by, from delivery men to wine buffs, is offered a glass of wine. Here wine is social glue, not just a commodity.

Franco Toros checking the vines before the harvest

Sauvignon grapes

Toros is a fourth-generation grower who is already being joined at the winery by his three daughters. As a young man his father had him earmarked for a baker, but Franco soon got bored with bread and turned his attention to helping the family farm make better wine.

'A local priest has done research and discovered that our house is one of the area's oldest,' he says. 'Indeed, its small original cellar is dated 1648, so it seems wine has long been made here.' Other parts of the cellar were once used to stable animals. Toros' great-great-grandfather bought what had formerly been a noble family's hunting lodge and ran it as a mixed farm, producing cherries, peaches and vegetables as well as grapes. Over time the other fruits and crops were eliminated. The Toros now have ten hectares planted to vines, with some woods and pastures for a total of fifteen. The estate produces 70,000 bottles in all, between Tocai Friulano, Pinot Grigio, Pinot Bianco, Chardonnay and Sauvignon, as well as a fine Merlot that comes out after three years following 30 months of barrel ageing, and that won him his first Tre Bicchieri award in 1997.

Toros is considered a classicist. His wines are known for their clean elegance; they remain fresh and easy to drink without losing character. While almost all of the white grapes are worked in steel using home-selected yeasts, Toros has recently added complexity to his single-varietal white line by fermenting small amounts of the grapes – from 15 to 20% depending on the variety – in barriques. These batches are added to the rest after five months to help round out and stabilize the wines. Toros allows his Tocai Friulano grapes to attain complete maturity and to turn almost brown before hand-picking. This translates into a wine that retains notes of warm fruity ripeness and soft bitterness, with a vibrant minerality that leaves you wanting more.

'These results come down to the radical change in our approach to the countryside over the last thirty years,' he says. 'We all used to have mixed farms – ours was known for its soft fruit – where the vines were pushed like workhorses to produce 80 to 100 hectolitres of wine per hectare. Now, we work that same hectare of vineyard to produce a mere 30 hectolitres. We also go through each vineyard at least five times by hand during the course of the year, pruning, selecting, adjusting the leaf canopy. That's where the difference in quality really lies.'

As we return to the cellar after visiting the vineyards he says: 'I'm so happy to live surrounded by my vines. That's our winning card: whereas many big wineries buy in grapes and adjust their wines in the cellars, small, family run estates like ours are proud to be able to show off our vineyards, and invite people into our cellars and homes. We have nothing to hide. Now, won't you have a glass of wine?'

Brazzano

Brazzano is a small group of houses along the main road between Cormòns and Dolegna del Collio. Its vineyards are on the steep slopes to the east of this road. Tocai Friulano thrives here, as do other grapes that appreciate the long exposure to the sun that Brazzano's vineyards receive.

Restaurant, Agriturismo, Wine Shop
Osteria Terra & Vini

Via XXIV Maggio, 34
Brazzano
Tel 0481 60028
www.terraevini.it
PRICE €€-€€€

Across the main road through Brazzano from Livio Felluga's cellars, on a slight diagonal, is the family's lovely informal restaurant, Terra & Vini, overseen by Livio's daughter, Elda. It's a popular meeting place for local wine enthusiasts and makers who enjoy savouring a nice bottle accompanied by the uncomplicated country food on offer. In summer there are tables out in the quiet garden that is ovelooked by the agriturismo's seven rooms.

Terra & Vini

The menu changes daily, which ensures it is always fresh, seasonal and local, with spring field greens giving way to summer vegetables and autumn mushrooms, accompanied by roast meats, excellent local *salumi* and artisan cheeses. The desserts are home-made. Wines are drawn from the region and beyond, and are on offer by the glass or bottle; they are on sale in the shop next door too.

*The ageing cellar at
Borgo del Tiglio*

Wine

Via San Giorgio, 71
Brazzano
TEL 0481 62166
borgodeltiglio@libero.it

Borgo del Tiglio

Aesthetics matter. For someone like me, brought up in London
but also in the unspoiled countryside of the Cotswolds, where
rural buildings and their dry-stone walls were considered precious artefacts and were carefully restored, Borgo del Tiglio
holds a special fascination. I love the beauty of the old farmhouse with its imperfect, time-worn walls and sheltered courtyard, the neat stacks of firewood, the wrought-iron gate and the
hand-embroidered curtains. The simplicity that borders on aus-
terity is as rich in emotion as any place I've visited in the Collio.
Most of all I love to climb slowly up behind the cellars to the
high steep vineyard, Ronco delle Chiesa, with its twisted, sculptural vines of Tocai. This cast of characters was planted in the
1960s, and has been nurtured too, with grass and wildflowers
grown underfoot. It rewards by giving grapes of a richness and
complexity that only age and experience can confer.

Nicola Manferrari

All this is the work of Nicola Manferrari, a former pharma-
cist who, since 1981, has been the driving force behind this
exceptional winery and 8.5 hectares of vineyards, situated on
land bought by his father in the 1970s and by him in the 1980s.
His vision is as noticeably different for his wines as it is for his
house. Manferrari's viticultural inspiration and sensibilities
come more from France than Friuli, though Friulano he most
certainly is. 'In France there is a respect for the knowledge of
the past,' he says as we sit at the well-used wooden table in his
tasting room. 'To me, the most important patrimony we have in
Italy is the culture of the poor, of the 'unschooled' *contadini* and
artisans who seemingly have nothing to teach us but in fact
are the transmitters of our most significant wisdom. Look at

Tocai Friulano grapes on the old vines at Ronco della Chiesa

Palladio, who started life as a humble 16th-century builder and became one of the most influential architects in the world: he figured it all out for himself. In the countryside, it's the same: you can trace the history of an old vine if you know how to 'read' it: see that it was planted well fifty years ago by someone who understood its needs, but then hacked back in the 1970s when viticulture became a university subject and the experience of the *contadini* was lost.'

Manferrari notes that the parameters for making wine in the Collio have changed dramatically over three decades: from being inspired initially by the technology behind crisp, German white wines, the area has moved to embrace the long macerations and oxidisation of the Oslavia winemakers. 'Through all these changes my models have remained the Collio pioneers and Burgundy, where the wise use of barriques can add complexity, length and harmony to a wine.'

Manferrari is a stickler in the vineyards: whichever of his three parcels they come from, the grapes must be perfect when they come into the cellar: 'Our job is to pull the perfumes out of the grapes, and each vineyard must be worked individually to this end.' The aim? 'To make aromatic wines of flavour and equilibrium that will age well. A classic ideal. Tocai has to be saved from producing coarse wines; it's not easy to render them more elegant and fine. It all comes back to the character of the vintage and to the vineyards, to the specific bit of terroir on which those vines have been planted. If you get that right, you've got a chance of making a great wine.'

And make them he does, from the pure Collio Tocai Friulano that is focused on elegant fruit and fine length; to the more complex, seductive Tocai Friulano cru, Ronco della Chiesa, whose roots dig deep for their minerality, underpinned by the soft spice of the wood, and which improves with time; to the feminine, floral Malvasia Istriana, with its delicate caramel and spiced notes and crisp salinity; to Studio di Bianco, of Tocai, Sauvignon and Riesling Renano fermented and aged in barriques… the list includes Collio Chardonnay as well as Merlot. These are all wines to savour slowly, both as you drink them and as you cellar them: they never fear the test of time.

Wine

Via Risorgimento, 1
Brazzano
TEL 0481 60203
www.liviofelluga.it

Livio Felluga

Take just one step into Livio Felluga's elegant reception rooms at his Brazzano cellar and you are instantly struck by their modernist, quasi oriental style, so different from other wineries in the Collio. 'My father's family lost all its traditional properties after the Second World War, so we felt free to start from scratch,' explains Andrea, Livio's son, who now runs the estate with his siblings, Maurizio, Elda and Filippo. The chipper Livio, who is in his mid-nineties, still oversees operations and is very much the soul of the estate, but the younger generation has taken the reins of the business, day to day.

Livio Felluga is now the Collio's elder statesman and has long been a standard bearer for Friuli's wines. The eldest of seven children (his brother, Marco, see p. 223, is more than a decade his junior), Livio was born into a wine family at Isola d'Istria. He grew up in Grado, where his father, Giovanni, moved to distribute imported Istrian wines in what was the former Austro-

Andrea and Livio Felluga

*Opposite: Zorzon
vineyards below the
church of San Lorenzo*

Hungarian summer resort town. Captured in north Africa during the Second World War, Livio spent several years as a prisoner in Scotland; for some time his mother didn't know he was alive. When he returned to Italy in 1950, he decided to go on making wines in the family tradition. He bought vineyards in Rosazzo (in the Colli Orientali del Friuli), at Brazzano and Dolegna del Collio. The estate has since expanded to 200 hectares, of which 15 are in the Collio, including at Ruttars. The Fellugas are aided in their winemaking by the Tuscan œnologist Stefano Chioccioli.

Livio Felluga's wines and their labels have long been iconic symbols of Italy's best white wines. His 'carta geografica', or map label was avant-garde when it first came out in 1956. Using a beautiful hand-drawn 16th-century map, it pinpointed the hills around Cormòns from which the wines originated. This was before the creation of the Collio DOC, and it helped identify that part of Friuli as a great terroir for white wines. 'The wines were revolutionary as much for their content as for their image,' explains Andrea, as we taste a pure, fruit-driven Pinot Grigio from a recent vintage. 'Livio abandoned long macerations in favour of elegance and aromatic complexity, and has been recognized as one of the inventors of modern Italian white wine.' His portfolio of whites and reds includes: Terre Alte, a fine blend of Friulano, Sauvignon and Pinot Bianco from vineyards at Rosazzo, another of Livio's trend-setting wines for its purity and complexity; and Rosenplatz, Livio Felluga's Collio Bianco blend, of Sauvignon, Chardonnay and Pinot Grigio, lightly macerated and barrel-aged. For decades Livio travelled far and wide with his wines, introducing the Americans to Friuli's then little-known specialities.

Today, Livio doesn't often venture far beyond his home above the cellar or his daughter's osteria across the road, Terra & Vini (see p. 176). He's still clear on the concepts that brought him fame and success. 'The earth knows how to give us its fruits if we treat it – and each other – well,' he says, with the straight-talking wisdom of his great age. 'It deserves our respect. In wine, the only thing that matters is: *Qualità! Qualità! Qualità!*'

Wine, Agriturismo
Cantina Zorzon

Via Sottomonte, 75
Brazzano
TEL 0481 62398
www.zorzon.it
www.domus-rustica.it

Giorgio Deganis represents the third generation of his family's winemaking estate. 'I studied farming at Cividale and had always loved helping my maternal grandfather here when I was a child,' says the 35-year-old. 'Luigi Zorzon was born when these lands were under the Austro–Hungarian empire. He ran a

*Alda and Renato
Deganis*

*Petra Lind and Giorgio
Deganis*

food shop in the village, and owned this property and a few houses. When he died, in 1988, I came back to help my parents and run the business.' Giorgio's father, Renato Deganis, was a colonel in the army but loved the countryside, and has worked on the farm with his wife, Alda Zorzon, since he retired. The property was given an overhaul: vineyards from the mid-sixties were brought up to date; the cellar was modernized and an agriturismo was created. 'In 1970, when the *mezzadria* (sharecropping system) was disbanded, my grandfather offered the tenants the possibility to stay on as free workers. By the 1980s they had mostly retired, leaving their houses empty. My Austrian partner, Petra Lind, and I now run a bed and breakfast called Domus Rustica in those converted lodgings above the cellar.' There are two guest rooms and one apartment. Some overlook the church of San Lorenzo above Brazzano, which appears on the Zorzons' labels.

For Giorgio, Tocai Friulano is the quintessential Friuli wine. 'Go into any bar or osteria and you'll find people drinking it,' he says. Of the Zorzon's seven-plus hectares of vineyards, half are planted to the Tocai Friulano that has always been associated with Brazzano. The Zorzons were among the first to bottle their wines, as a 1953 diploma for a 1952 Tocai attests.

Like some other producers, Zorzon does not choose to make a Collio Bianco blend, preferring to vinify each varietal separately. 'I don't see the blend as a territorial wine. I prefer to make the single-variety wines because they are easier to recognize and compare.' The family produces 25,000 bottles, of which 70% are whites. The farm totals 22 hectares, with cereal crops grown in the plain. 'Up until now the markets, especially abroad, have wanted Pinot Grigio, Chardonnay and Sauvignon. Sometimes I feel people drink Pinot Grigio more for the name than because they really understand the wine.' Many of the Zorzons' customers are Austrian. 'They have a sense about Friuli, and love to visit the producers and taste and buy the wines where they are made,' says Petra. 'And when they arrive, we are happy to receive them,' adds Giorgio.

Agriturismo
Thomas Kitzmüller

Via XXIV Maggio, 56,
Brazzano
TEL 0481 60853.
thomas.kitzmueller@
virgilio.it

In this old country farmhouse furnished with antiques, the Kitzmullers' Bed & Breakfast offers two double rooms with kitchenette in a rural, authentic setting.

OTHER WINERIES

Boris and Alessandro Aita
Via Dante 9, Cormòns; tel 0481 61555
Barbara Bastiani
Via Dante 93, Cormòns; tel 0481 60848
Franco Blazic
Zegla 16, Cormòns; tel 0481 61720
Borgo Savain – Stefano Bastiani
Via Savaian 36, Cormòns ; tel 0481 60725
Franco Cantarut
Via San Rocco 30, Cormòns; tel 0481 67359
Casa dei Pini – Eraldo Sgubin
Via Zorutti 6, Cormòns; tel 0481 60298
Gianpaolo Cociancig
Pradis 18, Cormòns; tel 0481 61233
Andrea D'Osvaldo
Via Dante 40/1, Cormòns; tel 0481 61644
Stefano Gall
Via San Daniele 23, Cormòns; tel 0481 61454
Grazia Gardo
Via Monte Quarin 53, Cormòns; tel 040 771821
Kurtin – Albino Kurtin
Novali 9, Cormòns; tel 0481 60685
Manzocco – Dario Manzocco
Via Battisti 61, Cormòns; tel 0481 60590
Polje
Novali 12, Cormòns; tel 0481 60660
Giuliano Simcic
Via Colombicchio 53, Cormòns; tel 0481 61160
Laura Srednik
Pradis 1, Cormòns; tel 0481 61943
Subida di Monte – Antonutti
Monte 9, Cormòns ; tel 0481 61011
Terpin Fratelli
Via Gorizia 22, Cormòns; tel 0481 60147
Umberto Tomadoni
Pradis 9, Cormòns; tel 0481 62341
Tonut – Gianni Tonut
Via Foro Boario 14, Cormòns; tel 0481 61275
Francesco Vosca
Via Sottomonte 19, Cormòns; tel 0481 62135
Gabriele Battistutta
Via Zanetti 1, Borgnano, Cormòns; tel 0481/67219

Chapter 4

West from Dolegna del Collio

From Ruttars to the valleys of the Natisone, Cividale del Friuli, Udine and San Daniele, and east across the Isonzo valley

This chapter begins with the northern section of the Collio territory that is bounded on the west by the River Judrio, and on the east by the Slovenian hills. The Collio is very narrow at this point – hardly a kilometre from side to side. We'll follow a course from the Castle of Trussio with Ruttars and Vencò, up through Lonzano to Dolegna del Collio, and from there to the northernmost villages of the Collio, Scriò and Mernico. A winding road leads up through the vineyards to Scriò, which offers spectacular panoramas looking east to Slovenia, north to the Dolomite Mountains, and west towards Friuli.

The chapter then takes off to discover some of the gastronomic and cultural highlights of the surrounding area: starting in the east, with the Natisone valley villages, where dairymen still make their cheeses by hand in mountain hamlets. Then on to Cividale, past Udine and west to San Daniele, home of some of Italy's most sought-after prosciutti. Finally it curls back down towards the sea, stopping in some of the villages on the way to Farra d'Isonzo, where the next chapter begins.

Opposite: winter-pruned vines near Ruttars

Dolegna del Collio

Wine

Lonzano, 27
Dolegna del Collio
TEL 0481 60034
www.caronesca.it
VISITS Mon-Fri, prefer-
ably by appointment

Ca'Ronesca

To get to Ca'Ronesca you follow signs up from the valley at
Lonzano, on a road that curves ever more steeply until it gets to
the top. From here the views open out over long sweeping vineyards that follow the crest of the hills towards Ruttars. In
autumn, these vines change from green to yellow and red in a
spectacular display. The estate's 30 hectares of vineyards are
roughly divided into two areas, with a large new vineyard being
completed in 2009. A voluminous modern cellar gives ample
room for the wines and their vinification.

Ca'Ronesca's owner, Alcide Setten, from the Veneto, leaves
the day-to-day management of the winery as well as the making
of the wines to Franco Dalla Rosa, who has been at the estate
for fifteen years.

'Our vineyards are unusual in that they are in large blocks
surrounded by woods, and they have high, well ventilated positions which favour the perfumes of the wines,' says Dalla Rosa.
Ca'Ronesca produces two lines of Collio wines: Classic and
Riserva. The Classic line is all mono-varietal, with each grape
type being given different vinification. The Sauvignon, for example, is grown on the shadier sides of the hill to keep it green and
cool; it is also never sprayed with copper, which tends to neu-
tralize its aromatic components. In the cellar, it is protected
from oxygen by carbonic snow. Ribolla Gialla and Friulano are
given more traditional approaches, with skin macerations of
eight to twelve hours for the Ribolla and up to two days for the
Friulano. In the Riserva line, Marna is a Collio Bianco blend of
Pinot Bianco and Malvasia Istriana, while Vino Senza Qualità is
a special Chardonnay made from highly selected grapes.

Visitors are welcome at the estate, preferably by appointment,
from Monday to Friday.

Wine, Restaurant

Via della Ribolla Gialla, 2
Gramogliano
Corno di Rosazzo (UD)
TEL 0432 753222
www.collavini.com

Collavini

The Collavini family have their headquarters in a vine-covered
16th-century castle surrounded by vineyards in the comune of
Corno di Rosazzo. The estate is large, with over 170 hectares,
divided between the Colli Orientali, Collio and Grave DOCs,
some of it rented and some owned.

Manlio Collavini is a very distinguished gentleman who
recently retired from politics. 'My passion for wine is inherited
from my grandfather Eugenio,' he says, as we take a walking

Previous pages: The changing colours of Ca'Ronesca in autumn

tour through the large, technologically advanced cellars. 'He was a self-taught man of many cultures, who played several instruments and had a passion for sparkling wines. Indeed, he was a pioneer in making hand-crafted *spumanti*, despite having little equipment or technical support in those days.' Manlio, who was from Rivignano, took over running the estate in the mid-'60s, before buying it in 1967 from Caternario, duke of Quadri. 'I realized early on that the secret for us to make good wine here was in the collaboration we could establish with the grower-owners of the small vineyards that are scattered throughout the Collio. We offer them the security that their grapes will always be well paid for, as long as they follow our agronomist's advice about pruning, spraying, etc. From our point of view, they ensure that we get quality grapes picked and cared for by hand instead of by machine. This is still a world of retired people who are able to give their vineyards careful, intimate attention.'

Collavini is a great believer in the native grape varieties of the Collio as a means of differentiation. 'We must get away from the 'international' varieties and New World trends if we want to assert our identity.'

In the cellar Manlio and his son, Giovanni, use a natural means of *appassimento*, or water-reduction, of some of the white grapes by stacking them in small, airy crates in a humidity-controlled room for about two weeks. 'As with an Amarone, this increases the sugars and perfumes of the grapes without needing to resort to concentrates or other methods,' Manlio says. Indeed, they also use this system for the red Refosco grapes. The Collavinis also produce a Charmat-method *spumante* from Ribolla, though this is not a wine that is included in the Collio DOC. It stays on its yeasts for 24-28 months, and then spends eight months in the bottle before being sold. 'This gives us very fine bubbles, without needing to add liqueur.' Collavini doesn't love wood, but says it's like adding salt and pepper in cooking: you have to get the dose right.

Beside the castello is a shop for buying the estate's wines and a rustic osteria for meals.

Wine

Fantinel

Via Tesis, 8
Tauriano di Spilimbergo
(PN)
TEL 0427 591511
www.fantinel.com

Fantinel is one of Friuli's biggest private estates, with over 300 hectares of vineyards, of which 50 are positioned in the Collio DOC between Dolegna del Collio and Vencò. Annual production is circa 4.5 million bottles, of which over 1 million are *spumante*; the Collio yields 350,000 bottles. The Fantinel head-

The view from Ruttars towards Vencò

quarters are some distance from the Collio, at Spilimbergo, and that's where I went to talk to Marco Fantinel, the dynamic young director of the company who is also one of the Collio Consortium's councillors.

The core Fantinel family business was originally in hotels and restaurants in the Carnia mountains. 'My grandfather, Mario, dreamed of making wine to supply them, and in 1969 he bought our first vineyard property in the Collio,' says Marco. Mario's three sons were good at commerce and built Fantinel into a large holding which now includes wine, a prosciutto maker at San Daniele, Testa e Molinaro, (see p. 211), a chain of wine and prosciutto bars called Pane Vino e San Daniele (see p. 208), and even a football team at Trieste. 'We all believe in working hard,' says Marco, who himself is a goodwill ambassador to the United Nations as a result of his work on developing spirulina, a type of algae rich in proteins and aminoacids, as a food to combat hunger in the world without genetic modification. The Fantinels donate part of the proceeds of one wine, a Merlot from the Grave, to this cause, under the title of Celebrate Life.

The Fantinel's philosophy about vinification is characterized by temperature: they like to start with cold – almost freezing – grapes so they don't have to chill the must. Fermentation is launched at 17°C with innoculated yeasts and continues very slowly til mid December. The definitive cuvées are done in January. The estate produces 70% white wines, and 30% reds. Collio DOC wines are bottled under two labels: Vigneti Sant'Helena and Santa Caterina. In addition to several red wines, these lines include whites Chardonnay, Ribolla Gialla,

Vineyards of Ruttars

Friulano, Pinot Grigio and Sauvignon, as well as a Collio Bianco blend of Sauvignon, Friulano, Traminer and Picolit.

Wine

Lis Aganis

Ruttars, 43
Dolegna del Collio
TEL 0481 639698
lis-aganis@libero.it

Claudio Narduzzi's story is unusual by Friuli standards: it might fit better in Tuscany, where professionals from other walks of life often buy wine estates when they retire. Narduzzi was born in Friuli not far from the Collio in San Giovanni al Natisone and grew up in Gorizia. He left as a young man to do his military service and then signed up as an international pilot with Alitalia. 'After forty years of living out of suitcases and hotel rooms, I couldn't stand the thought of travelling any more,' says the affable Narduzzi. 'My dream was to retire to the country, to stay put and make wine.' In 1984 he bought a small farmhouse with less than two hectares of vines around it on the top of a steep, south-facing hill below Ruttars. He has made a small but functional vinification cellar in it, and works the land himself. As far as the winemaking goes, he's self-taught.

'I've always been very interested in wine and how it is made, so I've attended courses and read up on every aspect of the process,' he says. Several large tomes about French œnology sit close at hand on his kitchen table. Narduzzi produces 10,000 bottles, with a little help from the winemaker Vincenzo De Giuseppe. 'Modern winemaking can benefit greatly from some high-tech equipment, such as cooling systems for the must and temperature-controlled vats, but beyond that it's all about producing good grapes and trying not to ruin them,' he says. Narduzzi is a large man, and obviously enjoys the physical challenge of working in the vineyards. 'I'm not in this for the money,' he says. 'I just want to make a wine that I like, and sell it for a reasonable price.'

He currently makes three wines, a Friulano from the 35-year old vines below his house, a Sauvignon, and a Cabernet Franc. Only the red sees any wood, in tonneaux, as Narduzzi prefers his whites to be expressive of the grapes' natural fruit. He gives the Friulano a bit of maceration to intensify the colour, and is proud of this wine's distinctive bitter almond notes. He sells well in Rome and around Italy, and has a loyal audience in his fellow Alitalia staff members.

The name of Narduzzi's estate is distinctive too. In Friulano dialect, Lis Aganis are mythical water-spirits said to haunt the Judrio and other local rivers. They seem to be a cross between witches, mermaids and washer-women, and the jury's still out as to whether they are forces for good or evil. Narduzzi's Aganis are undoubtedly the former.

Wine

Via Montarezza, 33
Dolegnano (UD)
TEL 0432 757173
www.livon.it

Livon

Ruttars is one of the Collio's most sought-after sub-zones, and the Livon family own a large portion of it: 50 hectares up at the top of the hill, facing both towards Slovenia and back down towards the valley of the river Judrio; they also own over 200 hectares in other parts of Friuli. Dorino Livon began buying vineyards at Ruttars in 1964, after years of working as a tennant farmer and selling firewood. 'The '50s were pretty dark years here,' says his son Valneo who, with his brother Tonino, now runs the estate, 'but our father was one of the original members of the Collio Consortium, which was founded in 1964. At that time, no one seemed interested in this area, but Dorino had an intuition about Ruttars and we are glad he did!'

Barrels of vinegar at Livon

Valneo and his brother were born into winemaking. 'When we were still in our twenties we took a trip to Bordeaux and were blown away by what we saw there: the difference was enormous between their quality producing vineyards and our "workhorse" vines that were intended to yield as many kilos of grapes as possible.' In the early '80s the young men decided to make some radical changes. They replanted vineyards, increasing the vines per hectare to 9,000 – which was practically unheard of then. 'If we were to replant now, we might actually come down to 7,000, depending on the variety, but it started us making wines of quite a different order,' says Valneo.

Today, the winery's output is impressive: 500,000 bottles from the Collio, and more than 1 million from the Colli Orientali and

Grave, made in collaboration with winemaker Rinaldo Stocco. The Livons now own an estate in Chianti Classico, Borgo Salcetino, and one in Umbria, Fattoria ColSanto, where they produce red wines. At Ruttars they are also making a variation on balsamic vinegar in an *acetaia* whose wooden window shutters are continually under siege from a woodpecker.

RoncAlto is a separate nine hectare estate at Ruttars the family bought in 1997. Its wines include a Ribolla Gialla and a Cabernet Sauvignon. Of the Collio wines, Valbuins is a Sauvignon; Collio Bianco Solarco a blend of four white grapes; and the single-vineyard Ronc di Zorz is a fine Friulano. As Valneo says, 'Tocai Friulano is never too acidic, it's smooth, round and wins you over with its aftertaste of almonds – and always leaves you wanting another sip: we Friulani are addicted to it!'

I was also very keen to see the Livon's herd of sheep and goats that have been given official residence at Ruttars but graze up and down the hillside with their shepherd. As you can see from the photograph p. 246, I found them.

The Livon logo is taken from a 1930 Erté drawing of a 'C', for Collio. For their elegant agriturismo at Villa Chiòpris, see p. 213.

Wine, Agriturismo

Venica & Venica

Cerò, 8
Dolegna del Collio
TEL 0481 60177
www.venica.it

The Venica estate has 33 hectares of vineyards and is situated in the northernmost part of the Collio, in a narrow valley that rises up from Dolegna towards the Slovenian border and towards one of the most spectacularly situated villages in the area, Scriò. From those heights, the vineyards open out onto the crests of the hills, with cool breezes from the Slovenian Alps to help create highly aromatic wines. On the way up this narrow valley is the single vineyard which produces Venica's award-winning Sauvignon, Ronco delle Mele. In it, old apple trees are interspersed with vines aged from 30 to 40 years, in the original mixed planting system known as *'promiscuo'* that has now all but disappeared in Italy.

'We're lucky to have these varied microclimates which undergo big differences in temperature between day and night, as that always helps maintain the wines' perfumes,' explains Ornella Venica, who handles the winery's PR as well as running its lovely agriturismo rooms. When I first met her, she was also president of the Collio Consortium. 'Being in the northern Collio is good for our style of wines as our grapes ripen later.'

Ornella has been an active and tireless ambassador for the Collio, so I asked her what it meant to her: 'The Collio has a

Opposite: Valneo Livon

Ornella Venica

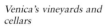

Venica's vineyards and cellars

strong territorial identity, is unspoiled and conveys a real sense of natural beauty and wildness, yet it's very diverse once you start to make wines here. The climatic or exposition differences may not seem that important to the casual observer, but they are the secret ingredients which can make a producer's wines unique.'

Certainly the Venicas have built their reputation on elegant, perfumed wines of mineral purity, with fine acidity well integrated into their structure. They are also long-living wines, lasting easily for five to ten years or more – especially the whites – even when they are worked exclusively in stainless steel.

This estate has been in the Venica family for 79 years, ever since Daniele bought the house and a small nucleus of vineyards in 1930. His son, Aldechi, was active there until his death in 2008, alongside his sons: Gianni is in charge of the administration and Giampaolo is director of sales, while Giorgio, Gianni's son, runs the cellars.

Recently, the Venicas have also acquired an estate in Calabria, Terre di Balbia, where they produce three red wines and some wonderful extra virgin olive oil, made following the precepts championed by the late Luigi Veronelli: cold-pressed without the pits, to keep the oil finer and less tannic.

If you're looking for a lovely place to stay in the Collio, the Venicas have created a very comfortable agriturismo for bed and breakfast within the nucleus of their winery buildings, with a private outdoor swimming pool and great breakfasts using local ingredients and home-made recipes.

Castello di Trussio, a Collio landmark

Restaurant

Via Ruttars, 11
Dolegna del Collio
TEL 0481 61255
aquiladoro@tin.it
CLOSED Weds, Thurs
PRICE €€€€-€€€€€€

Castello di Trussio: Ristorante Aquila d'Oro

The Castello di Trussio is one of the Collio's most photogenic landmarks. The fortified manor house dominates the valley of the Judrio at a point where the Collio is almost at its narrowest: Corno di Rosazzo is just across the bridge, with the Abbazia on its hill beyond. The medieval castle's structure was added to and knocked down at various stages of history, but today its 16th-century towers and imposing hilltop wall have been carefully restored. Trussio was in the property of the noble Spilimbergo family until 1869.

The castle now houses an elegant restaurant, L'Aquila d'Oro. In summer enjoy the panoramic garden terrace; in cooler weather eat inside in handsome dining rooms decorated with antiques. The style of the food matches its environment, with dishes well presented: ravioli filled with veal shin form the petals of a flower whose yellow centre is an egg yolk; beef carpaccio is enlivened with olives and capers. Risotto is a classic here, to be flavoured with the seasons, as is tender *guanciale* (veal jowl). The menu offers several options, from à la carte choices to the 4-course (circa 50 euro) or 6-course (circa 80 euro) specials. Giorgio Tuti's fine wine list rounds off the meal.

Other places to eat and sleep in Dolegna del Collio

The northern end of the Collio is home to several popular eating places where the menu sticks closely to traditions: thick country soups and pastas laced with Speck or wild mushrooms are followed invariably by meats grilled over an open fire and accompanied by local wines.

Da Vinicio (Via Zorutti, 20; 0481 60320) is set back from the road between Brazzano and Dolegna, with a large parking yard in front. Fabiano Bodigoi's rustic eating house is always full of families and large groups of friends or travellers who enjoy its relaxed environment and large portions. Choose from wines made by the owners or by local Collio producers.

Drive north through Dolegna del Collio towards Prepotto and you come, after a couple of minutes, to the small cluster of houses known as **Mernico**. Here there are two country trattorie:

Al Cjant dal Rusignûl Trattoria (Mernico, 8/1; tel 0481 639966. www.ferrucciosgubin.it), is a warm rustic style trattoria serving traditional local dishes with an occasional modernising twist. The Sgubin family also offer their guests rooms in La Casa degli Ospiti.

Grilled meats are trattoria favourites in the Collio

Trattoria Ferrighini (Via Mernico, 7; tel 0481 60549) is just beyond it, after the big bend in the road. This large trattoria was first opened in 1871 and is dominated by the huge fireplaces on which Giovanni Ferreghini grills the meats – from sausages to steaks – that he is known for. He and his young wife have an extensive list of pastas and soups; they have recently refurbished the dining rooms and the atmosphere is cheery and the food down-home, abundant and affordable.

Crastin (Ruttars, 33; tel 0481 630310). Sergio Collarig's agriturismo is open only at weekends and offers home-made wine accompanied by platters of ham and cheese from a panoramic position at Ruttars, one of the Collio's most sought-after crus.

Il Rustico (Ruttars, 39; tel 0481 60804) is also at Ruttars in a lovely stone building with fabulous views. Luca Persoglia makes his own wine here and serves home-made food, hot and cold, from the local repertoire.

Scriò is a tiny village that I adore: it's perched on the top of a high hill with wonderful views of the vineyards and Slovenia below, and offers a lovely place to stop for lunch or dinner with traditional food: **Ristorante Da Sgubin** (Scriò; tel 0481 60371).

The valley of the River Natisone

This important river valley leads with its confluents down from the Giulian Alps to the Isonzo Valley, and from there to the sea. Along its steep sides are woods, fields and stone villages where time seems to have stood still for fifty if not for a hundred years. Here most animals still live outdoors, and tiny vegetable gardens give way to woods filled with wildflowers and punctuated by 15th and 16th-century churches. These were war zones too, with trenches along the borders between Italy and Austria-Hungary.

Opposite: The view west from Scriò in autumn

Cheese

Latteria di Montefosca

Montefosca is a handful of houses of stone houses high in the hills west of Pulfero, the comune to which it belongs. You reach it by following the road towards Erbezzo after Pulfero. It's very close to the Slovenian border, and to Monte Vogu. Here, at 700 metres, above the valley of the river Natisone, cows are fed on the grasses and hay from unspoiled pastures. Several milk producers have banded together to turn their milk into cheese, calling their dairy simply La Latteria. You can't miss it, it's right in the centre of the hamlet. Giuliano Cernet is the dairyman who, four times a week, makes the cheese from unpasteurized milk; he also has the most cows. I watched with amazement as he worked the coagulated milk cantilevered over an enormous copper cauldron, scooping the curd into a muslin net as if he were a fisherman. The cheeses are pressed before spending 24 hours in the *salamoia*, or salt brine. Ideally the cheeses are best eaten after two to three months, but Giuliano explained that the Latteria often sells out when they are just a few weeks old. This cheese is similar to Montasio, but is called, naturally, Montefosca. The fresh curd can also be bought for the making of *frico*, where offcuts of the fresh soft cheese are mixed with mashed potatoes, melted under the grill and served hot as a starter.

Always phone to check opening times before venturing up the mountain to the Latteria.

Montefosca, 85
Pulfero (UD)
TEL 0432 726241

Stregna

Restaurant

Sale e Pepe Trattoria

Pick a nice day for a drive in the country and head up the Natisone valley to this wonderful country restaurant in a steep village so small it has just a town hall, a post office and this osteria. Salt and pepper are the everyday spices we all know and love, and Teresa Covaceuszach's delicious food seems familiar even the first time you taste it. 'Over twenty years ago I had a new daughter and was bored with office work,' recalls Teresa. 'My husband, Franco, and I decided to take over Stregna's osteria. It doubled as a grocery shop but was already losing clients to the supermarkets in the valley. The osteria had always been the heart of village life, but now only fifty residents remain and almost no one works here.' They began by cooking dinner parties for friends; the food was a hit and the word spread. Teresa is self-taught, an instinctive cook with a true sense about food: not only its cooking but also its sourcing.

Via Capoluogo, 19
Stregna (UD)
TEL 0432 724118
CLOSED Tues, Weds.
OPEN Thurs to Sun eves;
Sat and Sun lunch;
Mon eve in summer
PRICE €€€

Opposite: Making cheese at the Latteria di Montefosca

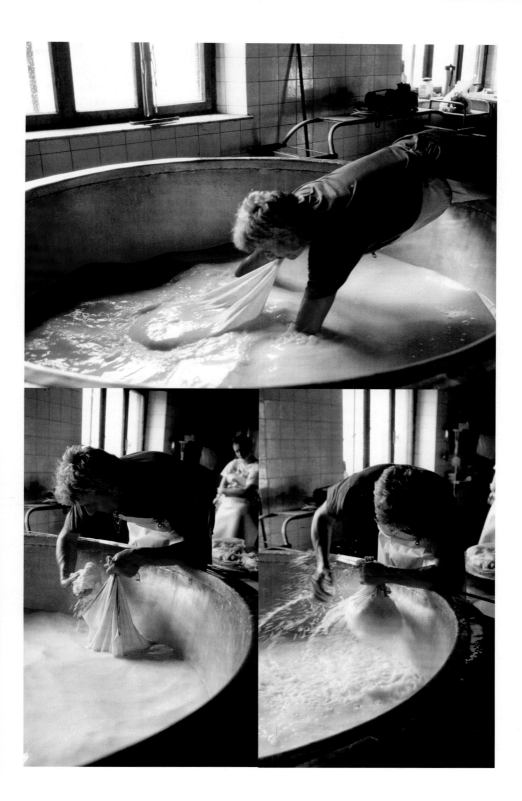

Teresa and Franco in front of the trattoria

Teresa's brovada soup

FOR MORE INFORMATION:
www.cividale.net

'I took a few courses, and that helped my technique, but what inspired me most were the memories of my grandmother's recipes and the taste of our local ingredients,' she says. 'What's great about a modest restaurant like ours is that we can get by with small amounts: we go foraging for wild mushrooms and herbs, and make use of game shot locally or courtyard animals our contadini rear. It's ever more important to be close to and respect the land we live in.'

Teresa began collecting stories and recipes from the village old folk. This area was never under Austrian dominion, but rather took its influences from Slovenia and four centuries of Venetian rule. 'Traditionally, many of our local women worked in service in the noble palazzi in Venice and learned to cook with the exotic spices they found there,' she says.

Vegetables often feature in Teresa's food: in autumn, a simple potato broth is given a welcome acid twist using pickled turnip *brovada*; in spring, savoury puddings feature baby-leaf field greens. A winter coleslaw of cabbage, Speck and apple has an original sauce of puréed fennel, cream cheese and apple vinegar. Duck is slow-cooked for four hours and given depth with a hint of bitter cocoa and chestnuts. Teresa's winter dessert, 'snow in a glass', conveys the essence of her approach to food (see photograph p. 38). 'In the 1960s, ice cream had not yet made it up to our village,' she says, laughing. 'So my grandfather would delight the local kids by scooping fresh snow into a glass and sprinkling sugar and chopped dried fruits onto it as a special treat.' Teresa's version sees a scoop of her own white gelato placed in the glass over spiced apple sauce, and topped with a fresh persimmon purée and a tiny poached Petural pear – an ancient variety that is only found in this area. It manages to be elegant and rustic, grown-up and child-friendly, modern yet true to its historical roots. You'll always find Teresa and Franco in their homey osteria, behind the old bar by the door, serving glasses of wine to the locals, or stoking the central hearth, the *fogolar*, that is the winter focal point of this very personal restaurant.

Cividale del Friuli

Cividale is undoubtedly one of the most beautiful towns in the area, and is a must-see for visitors to the Collio interested in Friuli's history. The medieval heart of the town, as well as its renaissance palazzi and churches, cling to the steep rocks overlooking the Natisone river which bisects it. The town centre is eminently walkable, and the best way to take in the layers of culture left here by the Celts, Romans, Longobards and

La Gubana

If you are a cake enthusiast the trip up to Stregna offers two wonderful village bakeries specializing in the local favourite, la Gubana. This yeast-bread filled with chopped sweetmeats and nuts and then coiled into a spiral is a Christmas speciality; here are some of the most sought-after producers of it:

La Gubana delle Nonna (Azzida, San Pietro al Natisone; tel 0432 727234. www.gubanadellanonna.com) is a delightful small bakery and shop in this miniature hamlet. The bakery was started by women in the village baking their grandmothers' specialities, and they still do: here the Gubana is light, dried-fruit filled and quite delicious. It comes in several sizes. The bakery also makes *strucchi* (bite-sized pastries stuffed with the Gubana filling) which are either fried or boiled; strudels, pies, tarts and cookies as well as some savoury tarts.

Pasticceria Panificio Qualizza (Via Merso di Sopra, 21, San Leonardo; tel 0432 723009) is in a tiny doorway of an anonymous house in the middle of the village of San Leonardo. The filling of their Gubana is quite rich, and retains the flavours of the alcohol the raisins have been soaked in. Strucchi and a lovely range of breads are also available.

*Cividale's monthly
flea market*

Venetians. Julius Caesar, in naming it Forum Iulii, recognized in
Cividale a strategic agricultural and trading centre; that name
eventually became the region's, Friuli. Over the centuries
Cividale maintained this status, flourishing in the 8th century
under the Longobards (or Lombards) and hosting the powerful
Aquileian patriarchs until the 13th century, when they moved
to Udine. In 1420 it was the turn of the Venetians, who ruled
Cividale for 400 years until the advent of the Austro-
Hungarians who, in 1866, were replaced by the newly created
Italians. The name, Cividale, has evolved from Civitas Austriæ,
and shows the importance this well-placed town had as a fron-
tier between Italy and Austria.

   Some of Cividale's extraordinary medieval monuments have
been highlighted by UNESCO, and are on their way to receiving
World Heritage status, including the Tempietto Longobardo, or
oratory of the Church of Santa Maria in Valle, and the Baptistery
of Callisto and Ara di Ratchis, an 8th-century altar to be found
in the Duomo's exceptional Christian Museum. Other important
sights are the Archeological Museum housed in a palazzo attrib-
uted to Andrea Palladio, and the Ponte del Diavolo, or devil's
bridge. Legend has it that when the high bridge was built, the
devil threatened to claim the soul of the first one to cross it; the
citizens got the better of him by sending a dog ahead of them.

   If you like antique fairs, Cividale hosts one on the last Sunday
of each month called *il Baule del Diavolo* (the devil's trunk) and
offers a fun way to spend a Sunday morning exploring the
town's central piazzas.

   Cividale also holds several important festivals and events,
including Mittelfest, an international avant-garde festival of
theatre, music and dance in July, and the August Palio di San
Donato.

*Cividale's Ponte
del Diavolo*

CIVIDALE'S FOOD AND WINES:

Scubla (Via Mazzini, 33; tel 0432 731995) Ermes and Moreno Scubla run one of the most important food stores in Friuli. Located in the heart of the town's curving streets, this is the place to stock up on speciality and local foods that have been hand-selected – and tasted – by the brothers Scubla. In the store's original 1920s décor, you'll find assorted olive oils, hams, cheeses, pasta, sauces, jams, artisan-made beers, Sicilian tuna and southern Italian pasta...a gastronomic treasure chest.

Pasticceria Gelateria Ducale (Piazza Picco, 24; tel 0432 730707) Stop in here for the best cakes and ice creams in Cividale. The Zorzenone family's pastry counters are tantalizingly full of cakes, cookies and pastries, including the famous Gubana, here made as the town's tradition would have it, without yeast in the dough. It even comes in a mini version, la Gubanetta. The gelato selection is abundant too, with delicious flavours that include both fruit and creamy ice creams. The shop is open til 9.30 pm daily except Monday, so you can fit in an after-dinner treat.

GustoBase (Piazza Paolo Diacono, 24; 0432 731383) This wine bar is located in Cividale's most central piazza, so it's the perfect place to stop in for a *tajùt*, or glass, of wine and a slice of prosciutto or cheese any time of the day. The list of wines by the glass changes weekly, and there are always interesting Collio and Friuli wines to sample.

Enoteca De Feo (Via Adelaide Ristori, 29; tel 0432 701425) Six tables and hundreds of wines: De Feo is one of central Cividale's most established wine shops/bars where you can either buy a bottle to go from the fine selection of local wines available, or stay for a glass of wine accompanied by a savoury snack. There is a limited daily menu for those wanting something more substantial, and tables outdoors in warm weather.

Orzano di Remanzacco

Restaurant

Ristorante Bibendum

Piazza Angeli, 3
Orzano di Remanzacco
(UD)
TEL 0432 649055
CLOSED Monday
PRICE €€€

You'll find Ristorante Bibendum in the central piazza of Orzano, a small village near Remanzacco in the plain between Cividale and Udine. Bibendum is in what used to be the village osteria and grocery shop: its stone walls and dark wooden rafters lend a rustic air to the quaintly appointed restaurant within. Barbara Martina is a self-taught young chef of some

Barbara Martina and Luciano Zuccolo

talent; with her husband, Luciano Zuccolo, she has created a personal style of modernized cuisine whose starting point remains the ingredients of this rural part of the country. If she has picked up on some of the culinary trends of the moment – slow-cooked, vacuum-packed meats, or syphon-formed foams – and unusual pairings from farther afield – cocoa and aubergine; mozzarella and melted butter – her best dishes take root in the classic flavours of the area: apples and pickled radicchio with tender pork; goose breast scented with saffron; browned dairy butter with duck liver. The couple's ambition is laudable: to create a low-cost high-quality restaurant – and they are well on their way.

Cheese shop
La Casa del Formaggio

Via De Gasperi, 31,
Remanzacco
TEL 0432 667056
CLOSED Sun; Mon;
Weds afternoons

Roberto Bruni is an *affinatore* of cheeses: he travels to all the small cheesemakers in the area and selects the cheeses he will then age slowly in his cellars. In his spacious shop on the main road between Udine and Cividale near Remanzacco, he carries on this family tradition with a fine range of cheeses from further afield: Italy and beyond. These are paired with unusual honeys, jams and jellies as well as local prosciutti and other makings for an excellent picnic.

Godia di Udine

Restaurant
Agli Amici Ristorante

Via Liguria, 250
Godia di Udine (UD)
TEL 0432 565411
www.agliamici.it
CLOSED Sun eve; Mon;
Tues lunch
PRICE €€€€-€€€€€

One of the greatest pleasures for me as a food writer is to return to a restaurant after a period of time and discover that the chef has, in the interim, found a strong personal voice. In this case, three years had passed since my first visit to Emanuele Scarello's Agli Amici, in the tiny village of Godia, just outside of Udine. I remember being impressed but not knocked out then by the young chef's cooking abilities: the dishes had seemed ambitious but not fully in focus. Scarello seemed still to be searching for that elusive mix of inspiration and clarity – anchored by technique and a great palate – that only few chefs achieve.

It's exciting to see what changes have taken place. Not so much to the restaurant itself, which is spare, comfortable and scheduled for future redesign. Scarello has risen in the ranks of the Jeunes Restaurateurs d'Europe, and his succession of brilliant dishes suggests a new confidence. In late September, my 'benvenuto', or 'welcome' teaser, a triptych of tiny receptacles containing variations on a squid theme, includes a sleek seppia *raviolo* – where the mollusc becomes the pasta – topped with black olive and liquorice 'charcoal', and a warm calamari-fennel pudding barely scented with smoke. *'Brezza di mare'* follows: slices of warmed fish and seaweed in a transparent packet unleash a salty-sweet sea breeze when you open it. Sweet again, almost floral, are the scallops sprinkled with Sevruga caviare onto which a hot potato-skin broth is poured; a sensual, simple yet delicious dish. Godia is known for its potatoes, and they star again in Scarello's *minestra* of white wine with gnocchi. The white potatoes are shaped into delicate dumplings and topped with morsels of sea urchin as punctuation to the ethereal wine broth. Scarello's diminutive mother, Ivonne, who has passed the art of cooking down to her son, still makes those gnocchi by hand and comes, late in the meal, to welcome guests at the table as if to her home. That's the other secret ingredient here, the hospitality of five generations of restaurateurs running a trattoria since 1887. The meal continues through courses of scampi paired with pork jowl, wild duck spiced with blood orange, and an inspiring white-chocolate junket fashioned by the restaurant's Japanese pastry chef. Emanuele's sister, Michela, is our host; she suggests unique wines to accompany his complex and, this time, unforgettable food.

Udine

Udine is a fascinating city with an historic centre that is well worth exploring. Although beyond the scope of this book, I've

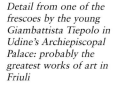

Detail from one of the frescoes by the young Giambattista Tiepolo in Udine's Archiepiscopal Palace: probably the greatest works of art in Friuli

The market square in Udine

included a mentionof Udine to encourage people to visit it.
The city is just 125 kilometres from Venice; indeed, for four
centuries beginning around 1400 it was one of the Serenissima's
most important cities, and today retains much of its Venetian
character. Its central Piazza Matteotti hosts a lively monthly
antiques market (on the first Sunday of the month) as well as
daily flower and food stalls.

If you get there, stop in for a snack and glass of wine at
Enoteca Pane Vino e San Daniele (Piazza del Lionello, 12;
tel 0432 505606). Run by Collio producer, Fantinel (see p. 190)
it offers just what it says: bread, wine and prosciutto from San
Daniele .

San Daniele del Friuli

FOR MORE INFORMATION:
www.prosciutto
sandaniele.it

Prosciutto di San Daniele

Friuli is home to one of the world's greatest hams and an Italian
culinary treasure: prosciutto di San Daniele. Although it may be
less famous abroad than its celebrated Parma cousin, San
Daniele's *prosciutto crudo* has what could be described as a cult
following in northern Italy and among discerning international
chefs and gourmets who value its elegance and sweet flavour.
It was considered a delicacy by the ancient Romans, the doges
of Venice and by French 18th-century invaders. You can spot a
San Daniele prosciutto at a glance: tradition (and, more recently,
legislation) dictates that the pig's trotter be left on the leg, so the
hams have a graceful pointed finish.

The small town of San Daniele, to the west of Udine, is
almost exclusively dedicated to the production of these salt-
cured hams. That's no accident: in the centuries before refrigera-

tion, ideal places for preserving and curing meats were selected for their natural supply of cool breezes in winter. San Daniele gets plenty of those coming down off the mountains. The little town also gets moist, warmer air currents up from the sea, and these are equally important for ensuring that the hams remain tender and do not dry out too much. This double exposure makes San Daniele unique, or *irripetibile*, as the Italians say.

The traditional drying rooms relied on manual know-how and sensibilities to control these air currents. Windows at both ends of the long rooms were opened to allow cross currents in as needed. Despite the advent of today's computer-controlled cooling 'cells', some of the *prosciuttifici* of San Daniele still manually open and close their windows to usher in the breezes.

Salt-curing meats is believed to have been first practised by the Celts in 300 BC. To make the prosciutto, the pigs' whole rear legs are chilled, massaged and then salted using coarse sea salt. The hams go through a series of phases taking several

An expert tests a ham for readiness using a sharp, hollow bone

*Opposite: San Daniele
prosciutti in the drying
room*

months: they are drained of liquid by natural osmosis, surface-
dried by cold air, and then allowed to dry more deeply for a
longer period at 4°C to ensure that no bacterial activity remains
in the meat. At this point they are washed using hot water to
reawaken the 'positive' enzymes, and then slowly brought back
to room temperature. During the process, the exposed part of
the meat around the bone is smeared with fat to prevent it from
drying out. The whole curing process takes at least 13 months,
and only perfect hams receive the coveted and highly controlled
DOP (Denominazione di Origine Protetta) brand. San Daniele
hams received their first safeguarding legislation in 1970.

Today, the 29 producers at San Daniele are members of a
Consortium whose annual output of hams is 2.6 million (as
opposed to Parma's 11 million). These are all hams of Italian-
bred pigs that have been fattened in eleven designated areas of
northern and central Italy. Nowadays, the pigs are reared
indoors, in large custom-built buildings as EU law does not
allow for them to be raised outdoors without special exemption.
Within the Consortium, some of the members (and Italian
supermarket chains like the COOP) are moving towards
improving the quality of the pigs' lives, by giving them bigger
pens and banishing genetically modified feeds.

I have it on good authority that San Daniele prosciutto is best
paired with Tocai Friulano wine, and always more delicious
when sliced by hand – but only by those who know how, as that
is an art in itself. I visited **Prosciuttificio Testa & Molinaro**, an
excellent traditional producer now owned by the Fantinel wine
family (see p. 190).

Mortegliano

Restaurant, Hotel
Trattoria Da Nando

Viale Divisione Julia, 14
Mortegliano (UD)
TEL 0432 760187
www.danando.it
PRICE €€€€

This busy restaurant is further west than most of the addresses
in this book, but if you find yourself in the area it's worth a visit
for the excellent local ingredients you'll find here. Ivan Uanetto
is a gentle giant who loves to eat and, with his brother Sandro,
he's selected the best polenta flours, cheeses, and other artisan
foods to accompany one of the region's most ample wine lists.
The men's mother, Isolina, set the tone in the kitchen by cooking
home-made pastas, soups and meat dishes that would satisfy
even the hungriest hunter. The key word here is abundance in
all its configurations, from local fish and vegetables to oils and
wines from Friuli and beyond. The family's small hotel allows
you to enjoy the meal fully without having to leave the area.

Pavia di Udine

Restaurant
Antico Foledor Conte Lovaria

Via Udine, 41
Pavia di Udine (UD)
TEL 0432 685010
www.villalovaria.it
CLOSED Mon
OPEN Weds to Sat
lunch and dinner;
Sun lunch;
Tues dinner
PRICE €€€€

It's courageous to create a restaurant for a maximum capacity of 20 diners, but that's what chef Antonia Klugmann and her partner Romano De Feo have done. They've chosen a perfect spot for it, a converted building within the large gardens of a noble walled estate, Villa Lovaria, which itself hosts a pretty agriturismo residence. The couple offer a choice of two set menus each day, based on fish or meat, each with six or seven courses; the restaurant is open for dinner only (lunch by appointment only). Klugmann's dishes are elaborate, as are De Feo's overly long explanations of them. Care is taken about sourcing ingredients and the complicated food is well prepared. In late summer, guinea fowl was elegantly cooked in an oil confit and served with chestnuts, tart valley apples, mustard vinaigrette and duck broth. A play on pan-fried, breaded *cotoletta alla milanese* saw the veal cutlet replaced here by a mousse of calf's liver *alla veneziana*, which arrived on a bed of cabbage accented with baked plums. If you come in the mood for a leisurely evening meal and great wines in a striking environment, you won't be disappointed.

Restaurant
La Frasca

Viale Grado, 10
Lauzacco
Pavia di Udine (UD)
TEL 0432 675150
www.lafrasca.com
CLOSED Weds
PRICE €€€

Valter Scarbolo's trattoria is like a wine bar with food, and it's always jumping. It's a great place to stop in for a drink – try the Bastianichs' fine Vespa Bianco, it's made nearby – and then stay on for an informal dinner of locally produced *salumi*, organic vegetables and home-made pastas. The grilled chicken or beef, accompanied by polenta, are classics here.

Buttrio

Buttrio is a winemaking centre with something of Wonderland about it: I can't help marvelling at its 1837 clocktower, with its inverted clockfaces – the 12 is at the bottom and the 6 at the top – how do they tell the time here? (Indeed, this isn't the only 'out-of-the-way' feature in the area. Alice would also have appreciated the giant chair that sits on a roundabout at Manzano: it's three storeys high!). Buttrio's Castello is a wine estate owned by Alessandra Felluga, daughter of Collio producer Marco Felluga (see p. 223).

Restaurant
Trattoria Al Parco

Via Stretta del Parco, 7
Buttrio (UD)
TEL 0432 674025
parco.meroi@libero.it
CLOSED Tues eve; Wed.
PRICE €€€

Vegetable risotto

I'm fond of this rustic-refined restaurant, with its contemporary feel in a traditional setting. It's located in a large stone country house just across the piazza from Buttrio's clocktower, and is run by Paolo and Francesca Meroi who are themselves great wine producers in Friuli's Colli Orientali. The energy of this restaurant is concentrated around its grill: a large open fireplace where Paolo, who doubles as winemaker and grill-chef, personally cooks the choice meats for which Al Parco remains a perennial favourite: slabs of pork, beef, veal and lamb, as well as sausages, mushrooms... anything grillable. Meroi also makes a memorable grilled chicken half that takes an hour to cook, but is worth the wait. Start with addictive hand-made potato crisps, sliced prosciutto, risottos flavoured with whatever the seasons have to offer, from asparagus to funghi, or pasta. And save room for dessert: the super-crisp frolla cookies with jam are divine.

Chiòpris Viscone

Agriturismo
Villa Chiòpris

Via C. Battisti, 6
Chiòpris Viscone (UD)
TEL 0432 991380
www.villachiopris.it

A recent project of the ambitious Livon winemaking family has been the renovation of one of Friuli's historic country houses, Villa Chiòpris, in the pebbly winemaking area called the Grave. It was formerly owned by Hermann Hausbrandt, whose coffee is a household name in northern Italy. Not only have the vineyards been given an overhaul, but the villa and its cellars have been converted to an attractive agriturismo with nine rooms, perfect for tranquil bed and breakfasts. It's even set up for wedding parties.

San Giovanni al Natisone

Restaurant, Hotel
Ristorante Al Campiello

Via Nazionale, 40
San Giovanni al
Natisone (UD)
TEL 0432 757910
www.ristorante-
campiello.it
CLOSED Sun
PRICE €€€€€-€€€€€€

This successful restaurant is located on the ground floor of the 19-room hotel run by the same family, the Macorigs, since the 1960s. Dario is an enthusiastic host, and has created a comfortable environment for their loyal customers who return often for the local seafood, fabulous wines – including many Champagnes – and lively atmosphere. He and his wife, Marisa, take turns cooking and have a light touch with fish, much of which is so fresh it can be eaten raw, *crudo*. Don't miss the pasta course,

*Aperitivo at Villa
Chiòpris*

here sauced with whatever is freshest from the sea. The menu
also always features some of the classic dishes of the area and
some meat for those not wanting seafood.

Agriturismo

Agriturismo Carvalho

Via Giassico, 2
Villanova del Judrio
San Giovanni al
Natisone (UD)
TEL 0432 758000
www.agriturismoberia.it

The beautifully appointed villa of Carlo Carvalho Beria, whose
full title is Marchese Carlo de Carvalho de Moraes de Puppi
Beria di Sale e d'Argentina, sits in a private park on a corner of
the main road from Brazzano to Manzano, at Villanova del
Judrio, surrounded by a high protective wall. (The nobleman
also owns the imposing Villa Beria at Manzano). He has done a
lovely job of converting the rooms of three stone houses beside
the villa, furnishing them with antiques and his sophisticated
sense of style. A lovely place to stay in the Collio area.

OTHER WINERIES

Michele Buiatti
Via Cividale, 8, Dolegna Del Collio; tel 0481 639953
Casa delle Rose – Maurizia Culot
Ruttars, 30, Dolegna Del Collio; tel 0481 630083
La Rajade
Petrus 2, Dolegna Del Collio,; tel 0481 639380
Norina Pez – Stefano Bernardis
Via Zorutti, 12, Dolegna Del Collio; tel 0481 639951
Alessandro Pascolo
Ruttars 1, Dolegna Del Collio; tel 0481 61144
Rino Snidarcig
Scriò, 10, Dolegna Del Collio; tel 0481 639900
Tenuta La Ponca
Scriò, 13, Dolegna Del Collio; tel 0481 62393
Braidot
Viale Palmanova, 24, Versa, Romans; tel 0481 908970
(agriturismo also)
Andrea Visintini
Via Gramogliano, 27, Corno di Rosazzo; tel 0432
755813
I Clivi – Ferdinando Zanusso
Via Gramogliano, 20, Corno di Rosazzo; tel 0432
753429
Valle – L. Valle
Via Nazionale, 3, Buttrio; tel 0432 674289
Ronco dei Pini – C. Novello
Via Valli di Carnia, 3, Amaro; tel 0432 713239

Chapter 5

From Farra d'Isonzo to the sea

Via Gradisca d'Isonzo, Aquileia and Grado, through the Carso Hills to Trieste

This chapter begins with the Collio wineries around Farra d'Isonzo and Villanova, where Monte Fortin, a hill of the same soil structure as that of the main body of the Collio hills, ensures the granting of the Collio DOC to the vineyards registered within it. From here we go on a gastro-cultural exploration to the coast, via the important town of Gradisca d'Isonzo. Passing through Aquileia, the second most important Italian city under ancient Rome, we get to Grado, the coastal resort of the Austro-Hungarian empire. And then along the coast through the Carso Hills to the marvellous city of Trieste, capital of the region of Friuli Venezia Giulia, and a fitting place to end this culinary voyage.

Farra d'Isonzo

This village earned its name from *fara*, which in Lombard dialect meant a family stronghold. Near Farra a strategic bridge built by the Romans over the Isonzo later gave many armies, including those of the Goths, Ostrogoths and Huns and Turks, a place to cross on their way to attack the Roman empire. During the First World War, large tunnels were dug at the top of Monte Fortin to conceal cannons mounted there to repeal Austro-Hungarian attack. Today the area is a peaceful agricultural zone making some very good wines.

Opposite: Courtyard at Tenuta Villanova in spring

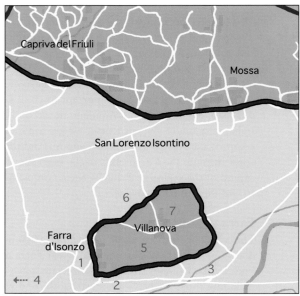

Via Conti Zoppini, 35
Farra d'Isonzo
tel 0481 888131
fulvio.bressan@tin.it

Wine

Bressan Mastri Vinai

Fulvio Bressan turns up to meet me driving an enormous cross-country vehicle. He is wearing camouflage gear, a steel-wire bracelet and a big smile. 'The Bressans have been making wine here since 1726,' he says as he points out over the plains of Isonzo towards the Collio hills. 'We found a reference to it in the old documents stored in the church at Farra d'Isonzo, along with the birth and marriage certificates. This was part of Austria before the First World War.'

Fulvio's grandfather, Luigi, had been the cellarmaster at Tenuta Villanova, and his father, Nereo, was one of the founders of the Collio. 'He invested in land when everyone else was selling it off, and kept a fine butcher's shop in Gorizia to support the winemaking here when wine was a less lucrative activity. He was the one that really turned this into a viable wine estate, inspired, as were many people here in the Collio, by Count Attems,' says Fulvio. Unusually for the period, Nereo planted native grapes Pignolo and Schiopettino rather than Chardonnay or Merlot, and trained them to Guyot instead of the more common bulk-producing Casarsa system.

Nereo is a great character and he and his wife, Paolina, still help Fulvio and his lovely wife, Jelena, to hand-bottle the wines and tend to the vineyards. He increased the seven hectares he inherited to 17; Fulvio has bought eight more for a total of 25; they are divided between the Collio and Isonzo areas though, by choice, none of his wines are labelled Collio DOC. 'Nature repays you for what you put into it with your experience, head and heart,' says Nereo.

'We have always opted to make less wine but of higher quality,' says Fulvio, whose annual output is now around 65,000 bottles. 'Initially my father was not very pleased when I decided to make wine after studying psychology at university, but now he is delighted as it has kept us all together.' Fulvio also studied in Bordeaux, taking classes with master œnologists like Yves Glories and Jacques Blouin. 'I loved the "simplicity" of these hugely influential vignerons who remain humble men of the earth,' he says. 'In Bordeaux I understood what great wines could be, I was almost jealous of the wines I tasted there, they were so good. Jealous of French experience and know-how that could result in wines like those.' Glories imparted the idea that you need to dream and imagine the wine you want to make, something that is only possible on a small, non-industrial scale. 'I'm after the soul of my wines and of my terroirs, their elegance, finesse and *tipicità*,' Fulvio explains.

Bressan wine in crate

Fulvio's first vineyard was planted to Schioppettino, as was the first vineyard planted for his delightful small son, Emanuele. Fulvio concentrates on autochthonous varieties, and allows them to age as in Bordeaux, *sur lie*. 'Nereo was terrified when I started doing this, as it was then a rare practise in Friuli,' says Fulvio. 'He asked me every day for three months if I knew what I was doing! When he tasted the results after the wines' long slow ageing, he too was convinced.' The Bressan's respect for the grapes allows for no pesticides or weedkillers in the vineyards and for wild yeasts in the fermentation. The grapes are de-stalked and lightly crushed, not pressed, before being placed in large, open-topped barrels to ferment and macerate. This method applies to both red and white wines. 'My Verduzzo is so rich it's like a red wine dressed in white wine's clothing,' he laughs. All of Bressan's wines undego the malolactic fermentation to increase their complexity. 'I love wines that evolve,' he says. When serving his red wines, as with the Pignolo, Pinot Nero and Schioppettino, it's best to open them early and let them breathe before drinking.

Wine

Casa Zuliani

Via Gradisca, 23
Farra d'Isonzo
TEL 0481 888506
www.casazuliani.com

Federico Frumento comes from a family that has made its name during the last 100 years in tuna fishing and canning at Marano Lagunare, on the coast between Venice and Trieste. Federico's grandmother, Bruna Zuliani, is from near Farra d'Isonzo and has a lovely villa that is now protected as a landmark building. Federico decided to 'rejoin' the family six years ago, after working for Fiat as a consultant. 'I left an active city life in industry to come back to the country here, and it's been quite hard to adjust,' he laughs. 'Running a wine estate may seem romantic but, at the end of the year, you need to balance the books.'

Frumento quickly decided he needed expert advice, and took on specialized consultant Gianni Menotti for the winemaking. Of the estate's 24 hectares of vines, half fall under the Collio DOC, the rest being in the Isonzo DOC. All the vineyards are in the flat, it's the quality of the soil that distinguishes one DOC from the other, a difference Frumento says you can see from the air. The dividing line between the two DOCs is at Farra d'Isonzo: here the Collio vineyards begin to rise slightly towards Farra's hill. From an old-fashioned system of planting, with 4,500 vines per hectare, the team have favoured a French style with from 7,500 to 9,000 plants per hectare, trained low to the ground which facilitates mechanized vineyard work. 'Despite that, we pick our grapes by hand,' says Federico.

Recent plantings have been to Malvasia, Tocai Friulano and a Cabernet Franc imported directly from France. 'We've discovered that a lot of the Cabernet Franc found in Friuli is really Carmenère, and is quite green and herbaceous, so we're trying the French variety.'

The Collio DOC line comprises seven mono-varietal wines: two reds and five whites. In addition to these is an IGT high line called Winter: a Sauvignon that is made in steel, as well as a Chardonnay and a red Bordelais blend that are both aged in wood.

Wine

Colmello di Grotta

Via Gorizia, 133
Farra d'Isonzo
tel 0481 888445
www.colmello.it

'This is my retreat,' says Francesca Bortolotto Possati. She's sitting out on the shady terrace of her country house, surrounded by pots of flowers and a lovely late-summer garden that leads directly into vineyards just waiting to be harvested. 'Living here in the Collio reminds me a bit of Napa Valley: you have to drive around to find the interesting things. Each village has one or two special foods or places and the fun is going looking for them.'

Ms. Bortolotto Possati escapes to Colmello di Grotta, the winery she inherited from her grandfather, Arnaldo Bennati, a Genovese shipping magnate, whenever she can leave her other thriving businesses: the elegant Bauer Hotels in Venice, two new projects on the Giudecca – including the renovation of a period Venetian garden – and the successful dairy she runs in San Canzian d'Isonzo (see p. 232). One of her most entrrerprising projects has been to become involved in a cosmetics laboratory in the women's prison in Venice that now supplies her hotels'

A canal divides Colmello di Grotta's vineyards

Francesca Bortolotto
Possati at Colmello
di Grotta

luxury creams for the customers and provides the women pris-
oners with an income and a job for their future. She is the director of Save Venice Inc. and also works tirelessly for cancer and
AIDS causes.

'I come from a family where women's entrepreneurial skills
were never underestimated,' she says. Indeed, her mother,
Luciana Bennati, first undertook the restructuring of this wine
estate, Colmello di Grotta, from the ruins of an abandoned hamlet in countryside that straddles two DOC winemaking areas:
Collio and Isonzo. She engaged œnologist Fabio Coser (see p.
171) to manage production. That was in the 1960s. Since then,
Francesca Bortolotto has overseen more modernisation, with the
help of Coser. Colmello now has around twenty hectares of vineyards. It was originally part of a much bigger property owned
by her grandfather that included Tenuta Villanova (see p. 227).

Francesca Bortolotto Possati spent many years in the US, and
speaks perfect English. She worked in interior design and has
personally redone the décor in her beautiful hotels. 'When I
came into all these properties, I felt it was my duty to come

back to Italy and take over,' she says. 'After all my grandfather and mother's passion and vision it would have been tragedy to let them fail.' She has done them proud, and her wines are now sold all over the world, including at the hotels. Her next project? 'I'm hoping my daughter, Olimpia, will come and join me in the business and guarantee the next generation.'

As for Colmello di Grotta's wines, they are divided between those made in Isonzo and the Collio. The Collio DOC wines include a line of crisp, single-varietal whites, of Pinot Grigio, Sauvignon, Chardonnay, Friulano and Ribolla Gialla, as well as a Collio Bianco blend, Sanfilip.

Wine

Via Gorizia, 121
Gradisca d'Isonzo
TEL 0481 99164
www.marcofelluga.it

Marco Felluga – Gradisca

Marco Felluga has spent the last thirty years as the spokesperson *per eccellenza* of the Collio. Not only as one of its most powerful producers, but also in his role as president of the Collio Consortium from 1999 to 2005 (he still retains the title of honorary president). His important wineries, both here at Gradisca d'Isonzo and at Russiz Superiore (now run by his son Roberto, see p. 117), have long represented this area's greatness abroad and in Italy, just as the Felluga family has ever been at the centre of Friuli's viticultural world. Marco's elder brother, Livio, runs an estate at Brazzano (see p. 179). The Fellugas' vinification cellars are models of modern technology. Alessandra, Marco's daughter, is in charge of the Castello di Buttrio, while another daughter, Patrizia, has her own winery nearby (see p. 95) and is currently president of the Consortium.

Marco Felluga has been instrumental in spreading the word about the value of the Collio's white wines – although he also produces some fine red wines. 'The Collio is really very small, but within it each zone has its own characteristics,' he says. 'The elements of our soils give our wines perfumes, minerality, body, acidity and elegance. I believe that the Collio Bianco blend is the most important standard-bearer we have: we shouldn't define how it ought to be made, it's best to leave each producer free to make their own decisions and create distinctive wines. One thing is sure: Collio Bianco is the pinnacle of our production.' Collio Bianco Molamatta is a blend of Pinot Bianco, Friulano and Ribolla Gialla. It ages on the lees for six months before bottle fining. It is made in the 60-hectare Russiz estate; the larger Gradisca estate is of 100 hectares. Of the estates' several lines, 'Marco Felluga' is usually mostly worked in steel and is produced at Gradisca, while the 'Russiz Superiore' line sees a percentage of wood-ageing.

Merlot grapes

Marco Felluga finds it positive that the Collio's sons and daughters are taking over from their parents, not leaving. 'This shows how much future potential we have,' he says. 'The change of ideas with each new generation is an added plus and keeps our wines at the forefront of Italy's production. The younger generation have also had to become entrepreneurs as much as winemakers. They've had to learn English and get their suitcases out to travel the world, as there's no doubt the wine world has become more competitive in recent years.'

Taking Pinot Grigio as an example, Felluga says: 'Many people think this is an easy-going grape making wines that are best drunk young, with little real character. Our Pinot Grigio is absolutely not like that, it's got distinctive floral notes, with good structure and a long finale. It sends a message that the Collio can produce successful wines both young and old.' Despite sharing the workload with his children, Marco still has the energy of a young man, and will no doubt keep sending messages himself about the Collio and its wonderful wines.

Wine

Jermann

Via Monte Fortino, 21
Villanova
Farra d'Isonzo
TEL 0481 888080
www.jermann.it

Silvio Jermann, like his father, Angelo, has long been a Friuli trail-blazer. Silvio's son, named Angelo like his grandfather, explains: 'Thirty years ago, when my father started, people didn't make the association between great wines and Friuli. Things were only just beginning to change and what counted most was a wine's brand, not its provenance.' Silvio was in his early twenties when the Jermanns brought out the first Vintage Tunina in 1975, a wine that was to set a benchmark for modern Italian white wines. This blend – of Sauvignon and Chardonnay worked together with the native varieties, Ribolla, Malvasia and Picolit – was rich in flavour and appeal, yet it was made exclusively in steel, and took a step away from the alcohol-heavy wines that were still prevalent in Italy at the time. Its extended stay on the yeasts added complexity and earned Tunina a reputation for longevity.

The modest estate that Silvio took over in the late '70s has expanded into a thriving, much larger one, with over 130 hectares to its name in three locations in and around the Collio. From their original headquarters in Farra d'Isonzo, where the Collio soil rises up out of the Isonzo plain in two separate hills, the Jermanns have recently branched out and built an imposing new cellar at Ruttars, where some of their most important vineyards have long been.

Opposite: Angelo Jermann

'Our new cellar is my father's dream come true,' explains Angelo enthusiastically. 'The idea was to create a cellar as close to the grapes as possible. It's a huge cellar, and although 60 per-cent of our vineyards are in the Collio, we only make about 30 percent of our wines in it.' Grapes from the four important crus are brought down into the press by gravity. After fermentation using only indigenous yeasts, the wines are aged separately in four rooms, each customized for its own wine in temperature and humidity. Capo Martino is a single-vineyard wine from Ruttars of indigenous grapes aged in large barrels: primarily Tocai Friulano, with added Ribolla Gialla, Malvasia Istriana and Picolit. It is aged in large barrels, with an annual produc-tion of around 16,000 bottles. W...Dreams... has evolved along with its name (it began as Where Dreams Have No End): it's still a Chardonnay selection fermented and aged in barriques, but Jermann now leaves the drinker to fill in the gaps. The third wine to be made there is Vinnae, of primarily Ribolla Gialla, with some Riesling and Friulano added, grown in the vineyards of Dolegna del Collio. The fourth is the celebrated blend Vintage Tunina. A more recent addition to the list is a Picolit, the first Jermann wine to be bottled under the Collio DOC.

In an unusual move, the Jermanns have been doing an expe-riment using a horse to plough the vineyards of their red Pignolo grapes. 'Some of our vineyards and fields are now grown organically,' says Angelo, 'and we wanted to measure the difference it makes using animal power as opposed to machine. The results are startling: we've counted that it takes a man using a tractor about 450 hours per year to work one hectare of vines. That same hectare demands 1,800 hours with a horse. The difference is that the horse fertilizes, and does not compact the soil. The French are way ahead of us in this kind of experience.' The Jermanns' pet project is a trans-border wine made using Pinot Bianco and Chardonnay grapes from Slovenia as well as from Italy. It's another step on the road to reconcilia-tion between the two halves of what was once a single wine-making area.

Wine

Strada Colombara, 13
Farra d'Isonzo
TEL 0481 888004
www.ruffino.it

Tenuta Borgo Conventi
Borgo Conventi is situated in a handsome villa that was formerly a Dominican monastery at the foot of Monte Fortin, in the Isonzo plain. Since 2001 it has been owned by the important Tuscan estate Ruffino. Borgo Conventi has over twenty hectares of vineyards in the DOC Collio area, with some above Preval and facing Monte Calvario, as well as around twenty hectares in the plains of Isonzo.

Sauvignon grapes at the harvest

It's threatening to pour as I go for a drive to see the vineyards with Paolo Corso, the resident winemaker who has been on this estate since 1989. 'In this terrain, all it takes is 30 minutes of rain for the whole vineyard to become water-logged and turn to muddy clay, so to create this five hectare vineyard we had to dig two kilometres of drainage channels,' explains Corso, as we skid along beside a sloping vineyard near Blanchis. A centennial oak tree perched above it makes me think of a landscape by Constable. They are currently replanting from three to four hectares per year here. Wild boar offer other challenges to the winemakers: 20 quintals of ripe grapes were eaten here over the Ferragosto holiday week by herds of the animals that are now considered pests in this area.

Borgo Conventi was founded in 1975 by Gianni Vescovo. 'He was a believer in wine as a vocation, seeing it less as a staple food and more as a hedonistic product,' says Paolo. These were the beginning years of the Collio DOC. 'Right away Vescovo planted up on the slopes of Monte Fortin, near Farra; he was also an early bottler.'

In 2001 the Folonari family, owners of Ruffino, took the decision to complement their portfolio of great red wines from seven estates in Tuscany with one in Friuli that could offer high-quality white wines. Not wanting to come in from outside presuming to know about this particular terroir, in 2004 they hired the local winemaking expert, Gianni Menotti (see p. 121) as a consultant. In addition to a fine range of DOC Collio mono-varietal wines that includes Pinot Grigio, Friulano and Ribolla Gialla, the estate produces three 'selections', of which two come from Collio vineyards: Colle Blanchis, a single-vineyard Sauvignon worked exclusively in steel; and Colle Russian, a Collio Bianco of Chardonnay, Malvasia and Riesling. Colle Blanchis' ethereal minerality and Colle Russian's dovetailed varieties are pleasant proof of the quality of this estate's top wines. A fully modernized cellar was built in 1990. It boasts underground presses that can receive the grapes by free fall and a vaulted *barricaia* for the rows of wooden barrels. The estate hasn't given up its taste for reds: they include native varieties Schioppettino and Refosco dal Peduncolo Rosso.

Wine, Grappa
Tenuta Villanova

Via Contessa Beretta, 29
Villanova di Farra
TEL 0481 889311
www.tenutavillanova.com
CELLAR VISITS
by appointment.
ESTATE SHOP OPEN daily

This large estate is situated in the plain just south of San Lorenzo Isontino. There a solitary hill, Monte Fortin, rises above its flat surroundings; its soil structure is so similar to that of the Collio that the vineyards planted on it are accepted as Collio DOC; the Tenuta's other wines are in the Isonzo DOC.

Giuseppina Grossi

The Tenuta's history as a wine-producing farm can be traced back to 1499. One of the Tenuta's current lines of wines is named for '*i mansi*', the 15th-century word for plots of land that appears on a parchment document from that date. The noble Strassoldo family were its feudal landowners, and wielded power in all walks of life, from politics to religion. In the 19th century the farm was owned by the Levi family who saw it through the transition from pre-phylloxera, mixed-culture vines to specialized vineyards planted with selected rootstocks. Alberto Levi had studied French viticulture and introduced Guyot training systems; he planted Merlot and other French varieties to complement autochthonous varieties like Refosco and Ribolla Gialla. Louis Pasteur came to visit and observe the vineyards. Tenuta Villanova was bought in 1932 by the entrepreneur Arnaldo Bennati as part of a much larger estate that included nearby Colmello di Grotta (see p. 221). Today, his widow, Signora Giuseppina Grossi, oversees the company's operations.

'Wine has always been a priority here,' says Renato Romanzin, the Tenuta's director. 'Of our 195 hectares of land, 130 are planted to vines.' The spacious cellars are equipped with all the latest equipment: computerized cooling systems for making white wines without risk of oxidization; barrels of various sizes for the ageing of reds and some white wines.

The Tenuta's nucleus of old buildings encloses a handsome shop and a lovely walled garden. Guests may also visit the distillery – one of Friuli's first. It was cited in a historic document from 1798 and today produces grappa from the estate's own grape residues. For those interested in more recent history, a steep walk up to the top of Monte Fortin reveals a warren of extraordinary cannon tunnels that were constructed there in the First World War as Italy's first line of defense against Austro-Hungarian positions in the Carso and Vipacco.

Museum, Restaurant, Agriturismo
Borgo Colmello

Strada della Grotta, 8
Farra d'Isonzo
TEL 0481 889013
www.borgocolmello.it

This small cluster of buildings contains an inn, a restaurant, and an important private museum dedicated to rural life, called Museo della Civiltà Contadina. Here the tools and materials needed for all aspects of 19th-century peasant life in this area have been lovingly collected, from early vine cultivation and winemaking to the breeding of silkworms, tool-forging and other domestic activities from local farms. The restaurant offers traditional food, or a glass of wine to be taken around the *fogolar*, or central fireplace, so common in old farmhouses here.

Gradisca d'Isonzo

This little-know small town is one of the area's most elegant for the central tree-filled piazza it contains, which resembles a park more than a square. Along it are the remains of the fortified walls that tell of Gradisca's fascinating history under several ruling forces: the Republic of Venice, Napoleon's French, the Hapsburgs and the Italians. For large parts of the last centuries Gradisca was paired with Gorizia as a single county, or *contea*. The town retains architectural examples from all of the above, and is well worth visiting.

EATING AND DRINKING IN GRADISCA D'ISONZO

Caffè Emopoli (Piazza d'Unità, 11; tel 0481 99441). Gradisca's historic café faces the central piazza-park with its lofty trees. This is the perfect place to sit with a cappuccino and home-baked pastry watching the Gradiscans come and go: it's their favourite spot to meet for a chat, have an aperitivo before dinner, a sandwich at lunchtime, or a cooling gelato in summer. If you don't want an alcoholic cocktail, ask for *un aperitivo analcolico* – alcohol-free.

Around the corner from the café, in a side street running perpendicular to the Piazza d'Unità, is one of the most important wine shops in the area, **Enoteca La Serenissima** (Via Cesare Battisti, 30; tel 0481 99528. www.enotecalaserenissima.it). It is Friuli Venezia Giulia's official regional wine shop, and it's located in the beautiful Palazzo dei Provveditori Veneti, built circa 1485. The large building has recently been restored, and the shop and wine bar now occupy several vaulted rooms on its ground floor. The walls are lined with dark wooden shelves containing selected wines from all over this large winemaking region. They are available by the bottle, but the enoteca also organizes frequent tastings and runs an active wine bar where many of the wines are on offer by the glass, accompanied by snacks made from the best local artisan foods. This is also a good place to shop for honeys, olive oil, jams, cookies, preserved vegetables and other delicacies that travel well and make perfect foodie presents. The collection is rounded off by regional grappas and other liqueurs.

Restaurant

Antica Trattoria alle Viole

Via Gorizia, 44
Gradisca d'Isonzo
TEL 0481 92630
PRICE €€€

This charming trattoria is located across the road from Marco Felluga's cellars and is, to my mind, one of the most successful of its type. Here the food is authentic, unfussy and – no mean feat – delicious. The restaurant was first opened in 1893 as an inn; today its country interior of pine floors and checked table-cloths is cheerful and fits with the food. In autumn, a pumpkin *sformato* – like a hot, solid purée – came with a delicate mixed-cheese sauce and *Carnia ricotta* grated on top. It really tasted of pumpkin. *Biechi*, the rough-cut egg-pasta squares that are a spe-ciality of the area, were sauced with venison in a well-balanced red wine sauce. Duck slow-braised with carrots, onions, sun-dried tomatoes and herbs was tender, and came with fine-grained white *polentina*, the aristocrat's version of coarse yellow maize polenta. The young chef, Fabrizio Cucchiaro, manages to retain the flavours in his dishes without making them heavy. A tart, fruit-filled strudel studded with pine nuts ended this lovely lunch. Collio wines are well represented here, and the host, Carmine Lacerra, is a friendly dining room presence.

OTHER WINERIES
La Bellanotte – Giuliani Guadagni
Strada della Bella Notte, 1, Farra d'Isonzo; tel 0481 888020
Borgo Tintor – Giovanni Bortoluzzi
Via Roma 43, Gradisca d'Isonzo; tel 0481 92250
This wine estate also has apple and pear orchards, and sells fruits, juices and jams as well as wine from its winery shop.

Ruda di Udine

Restaurant
Osteria Altran

Cortona, 19
Ruda di Udine (UD)
TEL 0431 969402
osteria.altran@libero.it
CLOSED Mon, Tues
PRICE €€€€

This large, cheerful restaurant in what resembles a country farmhouse has outgrown osteria status, in my book. Its rustic-chic, professionally run dining rooms make it a very pleasant place for everything from family dinners to more sedate business lunches. Owner and host, Guido Lanzellotti, runs a tight ship in symbiosis with his talented chef, Alessio Devidè. In early autumn, tiny fried red mullet fillets from the rocky Adriatic coasts are served on a delicious *zuppetta* of fennel and *semolino* – like a slightly grainy pudding – accented with red Venere rice. In what my food-writing friend and co-diner, Andrea Petrini, dubs the 'best sandwich of the year', roast veal sliced as thinly as prosciutto comes on fine layers of a sort of Melba toast, enriched with red wine reduction and cress; beside it are the sea-son's first leaves of bitter red radicchio cooked here in reduced

Opposite: Polenta flour and maize

balsamic vinegar. A rich dish of tagliatelle noodles follows, sauced with venison, Guanaja chocolate and butter. A grass-green soup is lighter: it contains squid ink-black and white ravioli filled with sweet peas. The chef easily stretches from traditional to modern dishes, and there's an extensive wine list to accompany them.

San Canzian d'Isonzo

Farm shop
Villa Luisa

Via Molino Rondon, 2
TEL 0481 482864
OPEN every day
till 8.30 pm

Villa Luisa is a model dairy farm. With 3,000 cows and 1,500 hectares of land, it is one of the biggest in the northeast. It is owned and run by Francesca Bortolotto Possati, who also owns the Collio winery Colmello di Grotta (see p. 221) and the fabulous Bauer Hotel in Venice. As in all things under Ms Possati's control, this farm's shop, or *spaccio*, is beautifully appointed and sells milk, butter, cheese and yogurt from the dairy, as well as meat butchered from the herd.

Aquileia

When Rome ruled the Mediterranean, its most important northern city on the Italian peninsula was Aquileia, which occupied a strategic military and commercial position at the crossroads of eastern and northern countries and the Adriatic sea. It became the capital of Rome's 'Regio X Venetia et Histria' under Emperor Augustus. Here a lucrative trade in amber was carried out with the Baltic, while glasswork, metal and wine produced by the Romans in various parts of the Empire were exported from the port. Spices and other rare foods were brought in along Aquileia's extensive network of roads and sea routes, as were slaves and other precious commodities. Celts, Illyrians, Greeks, Egyptians, Jews, and Syrians all settled in the city and contributed to its commercial development. Under the emperor Diocletian the town expanded, acquiring wealth and stature, as the scale of its public buildings demonstrated. Artists were encouraged, including mosaic masters and goldsmiths. A strong Christian community grew and drew upon the apostles' preaching; the bishop of Aquileia was endowed with the title of Patriarch.

In 452 AD Attila the Hun besieged and then sacked the city. Its Patriarch and people fled to Grado and to the islands around the Laguna that were easier to defend and thus founded Venice. Over the next 1,500 years, Aquileia's fortunes were to rise and fall with the vicissitudes of the area's constant political turmoil. It expanded under Charlemagne, who supported the return of Patriarch Massenzio; from the 9th to the 11th centuries the city flourished once more. In 1420 the Venetian Republic put an end to patriarchal rule and Aquileia returned to its origins as a simple agricultural centre. Today the Roman and other remains of its great cultural explosion are among Friuli Venezia Giulia's greatest tourist sites. The Archeological Museum, with its stunning collection of mosaic floors, statuary and other objects found in Roman tombs is unique, as are the Roman Forum, with its majestic columns and the important cathedral, which was built over the layers of Aquileia's fascinating history.

If you're in need of refreshment after all the sightseeing, stop into **Pasticceria Bar Mosaico** (Piazza Capitolo, 17; tel 0431 919592), across the road from the Basilica. This coffee bar and pastry shop specializes in chocolate. Mario Zerbin has long been a devotee of chocolate making, and has expanded the classic repertoire to include quintessentially Friulan inventions: chocolates containing Gubana cake filling and Aquileian chocolate 'mosaics' fight for shelf space here with fresh doughnuts *(Krapfen)* and strudels from the Austro-Hungarian tradition.

   Aquileia's other contribution to the area's gastronomic excellences are to be found in Flavio Comar's grappas from his family's **Distilleria Aquileia** (Via Julia Augusta, 87/a, tel 0431 91091, www.distilleriaaquileia.com). These master distillers are also unique in their artistic references: from Herman Hesse to Magritte, the inspiration for these sought-after grappas takes place in what they describe as the 'workshop of the spirits'. Of particular interest to this Collio project is the single-varietal grappa made from Ribolla Gialla, though others exist, of Sauvignon, Verduzzo, Cabernet, and Brunello, in addition to the Comars' fine collection of aged blended grappas.

Grado

One of the joys of the Collio – and one of the reasons for the singular microclimate that determines its viticulture – is the nearness of the sea. From Cormòns it only takes 45 minutes to drive to another world, to the lovely little island of Grado which is connected to the mainland by a roadworthy isthmus that juts out into the lagoon. Grado is also a fishing village whose strategic position has long made it a key player in the region. Grado was known as Aquae Gradatæ by the Romans who used it as a port for accessing their important city, Aquileia (see above). Over the centuries, as the politial situation changed around it, Grado was ruled by many, including the Byzantine Emperors, the Patriarchs of Aquileia, and Venetians, whose lagoon it shares. Grado offered a physical refuge for their rulers to escape to when invading armies threatened.

Grado was sacked by the English in 1810 and by the French in 1812. It was acquired by Austria in 1815, to which it belonged until 1918, when it was returned to Italy after its victory in the First World War. Grado enjoyed a heyday under the Austrians who developed it as a spa for its curative waters. Many vestiges of that 19th-century splendour remain in grand hotels and wide promenades by the beaches. Grado still operates as an important fishing port, and hosts a wholesale fish auction for locally caught seafood twice daily; it is known for its spring squid, which are fished from the lagoon. *Pesca turistica*

Assorted local fish at the market

(tourist fishing) is also available in some seasons, as are boats to explore the other towns of the Lagoon, such as Marano Lagunare.

Grado offers its visitors both the lovely beaches and shopping streets of its Hapsburg era, and the old fishing village, whose narrow winding streets are punctuated with churches and monuments of all periods, as testament to Grado's colourful historical past.

After a fish supper, wander down to the beach for an ice cream and coffee in one of the town's many lovely cafés.

Restaurant

Tavernetta all'Androna

Calle Porta Piccola, 6
Grado
TEL 0431 80950
www.androna.it
PRICE €€€€€

If you're in the mood to sample some of Grado's best seafood, in a cosy restaurant in the heart of the old part of town, you can't do better than Tavernetta all'Androna. The young chef, Attias Tarlao, and his brother, Allan, have taken over the family restaurant business. They are the third generation. Their father and grandfather, whose wonderful names were Narciso and Osiris, specialized in cooking fish, as do these generous young men. Androna offers the best seafood from the lagoon, the Adriatic and even the Tyrrhenian sea, for the menu's specialities of raw and cooked fish and shellfish. Venetian influences can be tasted in the classic *'saor'* preparation of sole and other small lagoon fish (in a sweet and sour vinegar marinade); more specifically from Grado is the *Boreto graesano*, a complex fish stew. Eat in the tavern's wood-pannelled dining rooms in cool weather, or out in the courtyard in summer. There are, as would be expected, many great white wines on the list here, from the Collio and beyond.

The Carso Hills

The Gulf of Trieste nestles against a long chain of hills known in Italian as the Carso (Kras in Slovenian) which at their northern end abut the hills of the Collio behind Gorizia. These two mountainous masses couldn't be more different: if the Collio's structure is diagonal layers of impacted marne whose soil crumbles as soon as it is disturbed, the Carso is made of pure limestone, bright white in parts, and hard. What soil there is lies in shallow layers on the rock which has over the millennia formed caves, deep potholes (known as *foibe*, and scene of some of the war's worst atrocities) and grottoes full of stalactites and other formations. The Carso is now mostly in Slovenia but a strip of it is Italian; its agriculture is quite

different from the Collio's. Excellent Carso wines are made from unusual native grape varieties – the white Vitovska and red Terrano – by Italian and Slovenian producers such as Kante, Vodopivec, and Zidarich, in cellars above the coastal road between Duino and Trieste. The Carso is also appreciated for its cheeses (of cow, sheep and goat's milk), olive oils and honeys made from sumac sap *(melata di sommacco)*, which has a slightly medicinal taste, with strong mineral salt, and wild cherry *(marasca)*, which starts sweet before developing a bitter aftertaste.

Cheese

Dario Zidaric

Prepotto, 36
Duino Aurisiana (TS)
TEL 040 201178
zidaric@tiscalinet.it

The natural grottoes hollowed out in the Carso's limestone hills make perfect ageing cellars for cheeses – if you can get down into them. Dario Zidaric uses a harness and mountain ropes to be lowered down into the vast damp cave 80 metres deep in which his cheeses spend up to three months to acquire their flavour. Dario and his wife, Sandra, feed their cows on hay and wild grasses grown in the Carso, as well as ground maize, sugar beet and soya. Their Friesian herd is in a large stable where the cows milk themselves using a robotic system that allows the animals to choose when they want to be milked. The Zidaric's cheeses are made with unpasteurized milk. There are several kinds: Tabor is a traditional Carso cheese, of *pasta molla* formed into rounds and aged for three months. Sandra Zidaric flavours it with wild herbs she gathers, including wild fennel flowers, and Carso savory *(santoreggia)*, a native herb resembling a long-leafed thyme.

To make Mlet, which means 'ground up' in Slovenian, rounds of Tabor are chopped up into small pieces and mixed with ground black pepper before being re-pressed into a cheese form. This aromatic cheese is then matured for three weeks before being sold.

Jama means grotto in Slovenian, while *jamar* is the person who goes down into the grotto. Jamar is the name of Zidaric's grotto-aged cheese; to make it, the curds are broken twice, at two-day intervals, and re-pressed with added salt. After two months in a refrigerated cell, the cheese is placed for two to three months in the grotto with 90% humidity; it spends a further month drying out once it is brought back to the surface. Cracks form in the cheese when it is dry-salted in this way, and the bacteria in the cave attack these veins forming a natural mould within the cheese. Twenty kilos of milk are needed to make each four-kilo round of cheese.

Opposite: Dario Zidaric and his grotto-aged cheese

*Autumn vegetable
garden*

Restaurant, Hotel
Lokanda Devetak

Brezici, 22
San Michele del Carso
Savogno d'Isonzo
TEL 0481 882756
www.devetak.com
CLOSED Mon, Tues
OPEN Weds to Sun for
dinner;
Sat, Sun also for lunch
PRICE €€€€-€€€€

The best place to sample the Carso's ingredients is at Lokanda
Devetak, a county inn and trattoria located at San Michele del
Carso, a village high in the hills between Gradisca d'Isonzo and
Doberdo del Lago (make sure you go armed with a map and
detailed instructions). Devetak is family run, prettily decorated
and very authentic in its approach to food. Augustin Devetak
has assembled a fine collection of local hand-made foods and
wines, from cheeses (see above) to hams and other *salumi*. You
can have a glass of wine and slice of prosciutto in the osteria, or
have a more substantial meal in the restaurant. His wife,
Gabriella, cooks traditional recipes with a modern twist, as in a
hot soup of wild field celery (*lustrik*) topped with a scoop of
olive-oil gelato and black olive paste. Prosciutto is sliced and
cooked in red Terrano wine. Game is often served here, as the
woods are all around the inn: in summer, roebuck (*capriolo*) is
marinated for three days with bay and rosemary and then
stewed with sweet muscat grapes, to be served with a confit of
Uva Fragola and rough-grained polenta. A savoury tart is made
of sweet onions and smoked Speck. Don't miss the spectacular
cellar Augustin has carved out of the rock below the building.

Piazza Unità d'Italia

Trieste   .

The striking thing about Trieste is its grandeur. The busy port, which spreads around the hills of a bay overlooking the Gulf of Trieste and Grado, on the Adriatic sea, exudes an air of 19th-century exoticism. You see it in the width of its promenades and the elegance of its official buildings, and in their architectural diversity. The Austrian imprint still prevails, with the added twist of Slavic and Latin influences that make for a much more interesting result. It's easy to imagine the lively cultural milieu in Trieste that attracted the most creative minds of the period, from James Joyce and Italo Svevo to Sigmund Freud.

The city's importance as a great seaport and shipbuilding centre declined after the First World War, when Trieste became annexed to Italy after the collapse of the Austro-Hungarian empire. Problems arose between the city's diverse ethnic groups. The Slovenes, who constituted circa 12% of the city's population in 1910, suffered persecution by the rising Fascist régime; in 1920 a group of Italian Fascists set fire to the Narodni dom, Trieste's Slovenes' cultural centre. In 1943 the occupying Germans annexed Trieste to their Operation Zone of the Adriatic Coast; the city was bombed by the Allies and hosted much Yugoslavian and Italian partisan resistance. Trieste was eventually freed by a combination of forces from Italian anti-Fascists, Tito's Yugoslavian partisans and a liberating army of New Zealanders. In 1947, Trieste and its surrounding area became a 'Free Territory'; they were divided into Zone A, administered by the Allies, and Zone B – including parts of Istria and the coastline from Muggia to Koper – run by Tito. The two were separated along the so-called 'Morgan Line'; incursions across that line heralded the advent of the Cold War.

Trieste from the tourist port

Trieste was to remain under Allied control until 1954 when Zone A was ceded to Italy and Zone B to Yugoslavia.

Today, Trieste's complex recent history is reflected in its multi-culturalism, which includes food. When the Suez Canal was opened, all the spices from the Asian countries and the Middle East arrived in Trieste, whose spice markets were legendary. Today, Trieste's Austrian café society eats in Italian fishermen's trattorie, buys their pastries in mittel-European bakeries and drinks Collio wines as they listen to the myriad musical styles competing for your ears. The city has recently been undergoing a lot of sprucing up and yet remains relatively unknown to foreign tourists, so this is a great time to explore it.

EATING AND DRINKING IN TRIESTE

Trieste is outside the central focus of this book, but here are a few suggestions of places where you can eat well and enjoy the surroundings if you are visiting the city:

One of Illy's signature coffee cups

Cafés are important in Trieste, as is coffee: this was the key European port for it. Illy Caffè is one of Italy's most prestigious and coffee brands, and the Illy family live and work in Trieste. Long known for their commitment to sustainability and to art and design, Illy also offers specialized courses in coffee appreciation at their **Università del caffè**, www.illy.com.

The Illy family is also involved in running **Expo Mittel School** (Via San Niccolò, 5; tel 040 3478869; www.expomittelschool.it), which offers courses, demonstrations and seminars on food, wine and local gastronomic culture.

If you want to sit and sip an Illy, **Caffè degli Specchi** (Piazza Unità d'Italia, 7; tel 040 365777) is located in the centre of Trieste's most exceptional piazzas, indeed one of Europe's largest. This historic café from 1839 is a great place to indulge in an evening aperitivo before dinner or leisurely afternoon tea with pastries. In fine weather sit out at the caffè's tables in the piazza.

Caffè Tommaseo is another landmark coffee house in the town centre (Piazza Tommaseo, 4; tel 040 362666). It's the oldest caffè in Trieste, and has retained its Viennese character in furniture, ambiance and pastries.

Villanovich is a super delicatessen, or *gastronomia* as they are known in Italy (Via delle Torri, 1; tel 040 631820). It's the most refined place in Trieste for buying artisan cheeses, fabulous hams and other *salumi*, pickles, capers, olive oils, honeys… plus all the makings for a gourmet picnic on the seafront.

If you come to Trieste by train, don't miss the city's best ice creams at **Gelateria Zampolli** (Via Ghega, 10; tel 040 364868) near the station. The tiramisù is a classic here, as is the caffè.

Opposite: Trieste canal

Radicchio comes in many shapes and sizes

La Bomboniera (Via XXX Ottobre, 3; tel 040 632752) means a candy dish, and this lovely turn-of-the-century pastry shop has all the trappings of a sweet haven. Visit it for the mittel-European specialities: strudels and krapfen, Sacher torte and Dobos, the Hungarian butter cake.

Enoteca Bere Bene (Viale Ippodromo, 23; tel 040 632752) is a well-established wine shop selling hundreds of great bottles including fine selections from the Collio, Slovenia and the Carso.

Enoteca Nanut (Via Genova, 10/E; tel 040 360642) is a stylish wine bar and perfect for an evening sipping wines from the impressive list and snacking on hand-made cheeses and *salumi*.

Hotel Design Urban (Via Androna Chiusa, 4; tel 040 302065. www.urbanhotel.it) is a small boutique hotel in modern style in the heart of old Trieste; very comfortable and central.

Restaurant
Pepenero Pepebianco Ristorante

Via Rittmeyer, 14/a
Trieste
TEL 040 7600716
www.pepenero
pepebianco.it
PRICE €€€€-€€€€€€

This is a recently opened, eye-catchingly designed modern restaurant in an ex-stable in the city's historic centre, so a perfect place for a stylish lunch or dinner while you're exploring the city. Owner-chef Michele Grandi has taken a tall, narrow space and used its height to advantage with colourful décor and a small mezzanine for those who prefer to eat from on high. The food is improving all the time: if the chef and his young sous-chef, Andrea Levratto, were just finding their wings when the restaurant first opened in the summer of 2008, by that autumn their dishes were already more decisive and balanced. This is a cuisine of pared-down flavours, modern technique and interesting combinations: monkfish tartare is accompanied by sweet-and-sour red onions, raisins and pink peppercorns; a miniature, rare hamburger comes topped with foie gras; porcini mushrooms are wrapped into square parcels with escarole, and seasoned with black olives; risotto is made with pumpkin and crab, then misted with balsamic vinegar. The team have come up with a great lunch formula: three dishes for less than 15 euros, all served at once: perfect for a quick getaway. There are more elaborate fixed-price menus for those wanting to savour this gastronomic experience slowly, accompanied by the wines of the Collio and Carso.

Restaurant
Scabar Ristorante

Erta di Sant'Anna, 63
Trieste
TEL 040 810368
www.scabar.it
CLOSED Mon
PRICE €€€€€

You'd never find this restaurant without a taxi or satellite guide, yet it's close to an exit from the upper autostrada above Trieste, in a high residential area of the city. The Scabar family have run it for many years, and specialize in the seafood cookery of chef

Amalia (Ami) Scabar, while her brother, Giorgio, takes care of the dining room and the wine cellar. The interior rooms and outdoor terrace, with views across the mountain, have been recently modernized. Ami is a wonderful cook, with an instinctive sense about how to work with fish without losing any of its virtues. Her daily menu relies on what the fishermen have brought in (there are meat or vegetable options too for those who don't want seafood) and usually starts with a selection of raw fish, *pesce crudo*. Here sea bass comes with lemon-ginger sauce; salmon with spicy pear mostarda; jumbo shrimp with fig compote; and tuna tartare with aubergine chutney. There are classic plates of spaghetti dressed with local shellfish, or tomato-bread soup paired with fresh anchovies. In the main courses, *baccalà* is wonderful with horseradish, as is squid with cabbage and wild fennel sauce. Ami always finds the balance in her dishes, and never lets technique get in the way of her sensual, delicious food. Don't miss the possibility of tasting some of the unique local wines here, such as those from the indigenous Vitovska grape grown in the Carso hills, by Vodopivec or Zidarich: they go marvellously with this food.

Muggia

Muggia is across from the old port of Trieste, on the southern side of the bay. It was once a tiny fishermen's village and still retains some of that character with modest wooden boats moored to a sheltering dock. Yet its main influence came directly from Venice, whose rule it was under after 1420, as a close look at the village's best architecture reveals. The main piazza of Muggia is worth a visit: it's a good place for an aperitivo seated facing the luminous quattrocento façade of the diminutive Duomo. The old part of town is overlooked by the castle of Muggia, which is now privately owned by artists who open it once or twice a year to visitors.

Restaurant
Trattoria Risorta

Riva E. De Amicis, 1/a
Muggia
TEL 040 271219
www.trattoriarisorta.it
CLOSED Sun eve; Mon
PRICE €€€€

On the dock, Risorta is a surprising restaurant. If the doorway looks less than promising, persevere. Inside you'll find a seafood chef of rare talent who steers a double course in the kitchen between his own cuisine and the popular seafood the Italians expect to find at the shore (heaping platters of spaghetti *con le vongole*, fresh clam sauce, or *fritto misto*, deep-fried fish). Stefano Blasotti does all that, and he does it well, but if you ask for his creative menu, or give him carte blanche for your meal,

Muggia

you'll be taken on a much more personal trip around the flavours of the Adriatic sea. In late summer, crisply grilled octopus (*piovra*) comes with a soft cream of buffalo mozzarella, tomato confit and basil oil; orange pumpkin soup serves as a base for red mullet topped with earthy black truffle; sea bass sits on a loose potato purée with a *guazzetto* 'soup' of porcini mushrooms. The combinations are limitless but the palate is clean and focused. In summer you can enjoy the foods from the waterfront terrace looking back at Trieste, with fine wines to accompany them.

Glossary

AGRITURISMO holiday rentals on farms or in country houses

ALLA BRACE cooked over wood embers

BARRIQUES small barrels, usually of French oak, popular in modern winemaking

BIECHI (BLEK, BLEC) irregularly shaped hand-made pasta

BIOLOGICO organic

BROVADA grated turnip aged in grape pomace

BOTTE large wooden barrel

CAPPUCCINA vine-training style now largely outmoded of single trunk trained to two arching productive stems on sides

CASA COLONICA tenant farmhouse

CASARSA expansive, now largely outmoded form of vine-training

COMUNE township

CORDONE SPERONATO (cordon spur) vine shaping style in which an old cane is wire-trained horizontally

CONTADINO peasant, farmworker, small farmer, or tenant farmer

CRU French term used in Italy to indicate a superior single vineyard and its wine

DAMIGIANA demijohn, large glass wine flask

DEGUSTAZIONE tasting (of wine or food)

DOBER TEK Slovenian for 'buon appetito'

DOC Denominazione di Origine Controllata

DOP Denominazione di Origine Protetta

ENOTECA wine bar, wine shop

ETTARO hectare (2.47 acres)

FLYSH layered Collio soil

FOLLATURA pushing down the cap of fermenting must

FRASCA informal wine bar, usually on rural wine estate

FRESCHEZZA crispness in wine

FRICO melted cheese with or without potato and onion

GNOCCHI potato dumplings, in this area usually large and stuffed

GNOCCHI DI SUSINE plum-filled potato gnocchi

GOSTILNA trattoria in Slovenian

GUYOT popular French vine-shaping style, in which a new cane is trained horizontally on a wire

INVAIATURA the changing of colour of grapes or olives

JOTA bean and cabbage soup flavoured with pork fat

MACERATION to leave the skins in contact with the fermenting must to extract colour and tannins

OSTERIA inn, now commonly used for informal restaurants

PALACINKA Slovenian dessert crepe or thin omelette

POLENTA maize flour

PONCA mineral-rich Collio soil

PRESNITZ fruit-filled Trieste cake similar to Gubana

RAZNJICI grilled meat skewers

RONCO choice hill for vine growing

SFUSO unbottled (wine), in bulk

SPUMANTE sparkling (wine)

TOC IN BRAIDE soft polenta with melted cheeses

TERROIR French word that denotes an area in winemaking

TRATTORIA a family-run country restaurant

TRAVASARE to rack or decant

Opposite: Miroslavo Keber working in the Renato Keber vineyard

Index

RESTAURANTS

Including rural agriturismi offering home-produced salumi and simple food, trattorie, and restaurants, both traditional and creatively modern in all price ranges

WHERE TO STAY IN THE COLLIO

Including a selection in differing price ranges, from Bed & Breakfasts and country agriturismi to more luxurious hotels

GENERAL INDEX